Basic Life Support:
Healthcare and Professional Rescuers

National Safety Council
Itasca, IL

BASIC LIFE SUPPORT: HEALTHCARE AND PROFESSIONAL RESCUERS

Published by the National Safety Council, 1121 Spring Lake Drive, Itasca, IL 60143-3201. Copyright © 2007 by the National Safety Council. All rights reserved. No part of this publication may be reproduced or distributed in any form or by any means, or stored in a database or retrieval system, without the prior written consent of the National Safety Council including, but not limited to, in any network or other electronic storage or transmission, or broadcast for distance learning.

12 11 10 5 4 3 2 1

ISBN: 978-0-87912-293-5

All photos © National Safety Council/Rick Brady, photographer.

NATIONAL SAFETY COUNCIL MISSION STATEMENT

The mission of the National Safety Council is to educate and influence people to prevent accidental injury and death.

DISCLAIMER

Although the information and recommendations contained in this publication have been compiled from sources believed to be reliable, the National Safety Council makes no guarantee as to, and assumes no responsibility for, the correctness, sufficiency, or completeness of such information or recommendations. Other or additional safety measures may be required under particular circumstances.

www.nsc.org

25M0410

About the National Safety Council

The National Safety Council (**www.nsc.org**) saves lives by preventing injuries and deaths at work, in homes, communities and on the roads, through leadership, research, education and advocacy.

Together with its 55,000 member companies and nationwide network of state and regional chapters, the NSC researches, produces and disseminates safety, health and environmental training and other educational materials.

The NSC's First Aid and CPR/AED courses have evolved to meet the changing needs of emergency responders at all levels of expertise. Upon completing a National Safety Council emergency care course, you will join millions of first aiders and emergency responders trained to protect life and promote health.

Author Acknowledgements

Many National Safety Council staff and affiliates have contributed to the production of this book and we would like to acknowledge the following people for their assistance:

Paul Satterlee MD, Medical Director, for reviewing and providing oversight of the content;

Tom Lochhaas, Editorial Services, for providing technical writing services;

John Kennedy, Group Vice President, for providing guidance and advocacy.

Donna M. Siegfried, Director, Emergency Care Programs, for providing vision and support;

Barbara Caracci, Director, Program Development and Training, for providing oversight of content, development and production;

Donna Fredenhagen, Product Manager, for providing marketing support;

Kathy Safranek, Project Administrator, for providing day-to-day assistance.

Reviewer Acknowledgments

Dr. Joseph H. Balatbat
VP Academic Affairs
Sanford Brown Institute
New York City, NY

Paul A. Ballard
Department of Kinesiology
Saginaw Valley State University
University Center, MI

Eric Niegelberg, M.S., NREMT-P
EMS Department
SUNY Stony Brook
Stony Brook, NY

Robb S. Rehberg, PhD, ATC, NREMT
Department of Exercise and Movement Sciences
William Paterson University
Towaco, NJ

Roland G. Rivera
NSC Emergency Care Program
Austin, TX

Table of Contents

Chapter 1

Role of the Professional Rescuer

Professional rescuers work in a variety of settings and have an important duty as part of the Emergency Medical Services (EMS) system to give initial care to victims of injury or sudden illness. The basic life support skills described in this text are a key part of the emergency care professional rescuers provide. Professional rescuers need to understand their role within the EMS system and the legal issues involved in providing care. Professional rescuers also often have an important role in helping prevent injuries and common sudden illnesses.

Basic Life Support in Emergencies

Although professional rescuers may also provide a wide variety of first aid for many types of injuries or sudden illness, care for life-threatening emergencies is most important. Two of the most serious threats to life are respiratory arrest and cardiac arrest. If either victim's breathing or the heart stops, the victim has only minutes to live.

Basic life support (BLS) generally refers to care given when the victim's breathing or heart stops. Many things can cause breathing or the heart to stop. BLS is often needed for victims of:

- Heart attack
- Drowning
- Choking
- Other injuries or conditions that affect breathing or the heart

Heart attack is the single most common cause of death in emergency situations, followed by strokes and injuries. In the United States every year:

- Over 800,000 heart attacks occur, resulting in 180,000 deaths.
- 162,000 die from strokes.
- 140,000 die from injuries.
- Almost 40 million visits are made to emergency departments because of injuries, leading to 2 million hospitalizations.

Table 1-1 lists the most common causes of injuries for which the victim goes to a hospital emergency department. Table 1-2 lists the annual deaths resulting from the most common types of injuries.

Professional rescuers in any setting may give basic life support for victims of heart attack,

Table 1-1

Injuries Annually Treated in Hospital Emergency Departments

Falls	7,989,000
Motor vehicle crashes	4,582,000
Struck by or against object	4,209,000
Cut or pierced by object	2,544,000
Overexertion and strenuous movements	1,686,000
Assault	1,608,000
Bites and stings (other than dog bites)	998,000
Poisoning (includes drug overdose)	750,000
Burns	516,000
Attempted suicide	438,000

Source: National Safety Council, Injury Facts 2005.

Table 1-2

Annual Deaths Due to Selected Injuries

Motor vehicle crashes	46,200
Suicide	31,655
Poisoning (includes drug overdose)	13,300
Falls	20,200
Assault by firearm	11,829
Choking	4,900
Drowning	3,800
Smoke, fire, flames	3,900
Mechanical forces	2,871
Assault by sharp objects	2,074
Bicycle crashes	767
Cold exposure	646
Water transport/boating accidents	617
Other breathing threats	583
Electrocution	454
Heat exposure	350
Burns	102
Venomous animals and plants	76

Source: National Safety Council, Injury Facts 2005.

stroke, choking, and many other kinds of life-threatening injuries.

PROFESSIONAL RESCUERS

A **professional rescuer** is a trained person who, in either an employment or a volunteer situation, has the responsibility to provide emergency care when needed. Following are some examples of professional rescuers **(Figure 1-1)**:

- Healthcare professionals: physicians, nurses, allied health professionals
- Firefighters
- Law enforcement, security, and military personnel
- EMTs, paramedics, first responders
- Park rangers, camp personnel, ski patrollers, lifeguards
- Responders in business, industry, and farming
- Athletic trainers
- Airline and cruise ship personnel
- Public safety and search-and-rescue personnel

What individuals in all of these and other settings have in common is that they are called upon to give care to victims in an emergency. This responsibility generally includes:

1. Having the training to provide basic life support, and staying current in that training.
2. Accessing the EMS system to ensure that a victim receives advanced medical care or rescue as quickly as possible when needed.
3. Ensuring the safety of the victim and others at the scene.
4. Managing the emergency scene and the victim until personnel with advanced training arrive and take over; assisting advanced personnel when needed.

A professional rescuer should also accept the responsibility to stay physically and mentally fit for these tasks, to review information and practice basic skills to stay proficient, and to act to prevent disease transmission to or from victims, others at the scene, and self. It is important to maintain a healthy lifestyle in order to be prepared to act whenever needed, and to be able to control the stresses that may come with the job.

Being prepared, in addition to having basic life support skills, includes:

- Having confidence in your knowledge and skills
- Readiness to act in a leadership role
- Knowing where to access a first aid kit at any time
- Knowing the telephone numbers for EMS (9-1-1 or local number), the Poison Control Center (800-222-1222), and other special services for your situation
- Being able to access the EMS system (cell phone or radio)

Professional Rescuer Versus Lay Rescuer

Professional rescuers include healthcare professionals and others who have a higher level of training than lay rescuers and perform more BLS skills. In addition, professional rescuers perform certain techniques in a different manner than most lay rescuers would perform them.

Figure 1-1 Examples of professional rescuers.

Professional rescuers follow the Emergency Cardiovascular Care guideline recommendations for basic life support. **This text presents all BLS techniques as currently recommended for healthcare provider BLS rescuers.**

THE EMS SYSTEM

Professional rescuers are often the first step in the **Emergency Medical Services (EMS) system.** In some cases a layperson may be first on the scene and may already be providing first aid. Someone may already have called 9-1-1. In many cases you will be the first professional to respond to the emergency, called by someone at the scene or by the EMS dispatcher. As such, you are often the first link in the process for ensuring the victim gets whatever help is needed.

The EMS system in the United States is a comprehensive network of professionals linked together to provide appropriate levels of medical care for victims of injury or sudden illness.* As a professional rescuer, your role in the system, in addition to caring for the victim until seen by

more advanced caregivers, is to make sure the EMS system responds as soon as possible. Call 9-1-1 (or your local or company emergency number), and in most communities in the United States, help will arrive within minutes.

The EMS system includes a number of different professionals with different levels of training and responsibilities **(Box 1-1).**

LEGAL ISSUES

Professional rescuers should understand their legal obligations for providing emergency care and other legal issues. Following accepted guidelines helps ensure that you will not be found legally liable if a victim does not fully recover. Always follow these general principles:

1. Act only as you are trained to act.
2. Get a victim's consent before giving care.
3. Do not move a victim unnecessarily.
4. Call for more advanced medical help.
5. Keep giving care until relieved by a professional with a higher level of training.

Duty to Act

As a professional, you have a **duty to act** to care for a victim of a medical emergency. You have accepted this responsibility as a dimension of your

---

*The term **sudden illness** is generally used to describe a medical emergency that occurs suddenly and requires basic life support or first aid until the person receives more advanced medical attention. This term will be used throughout this text.

Box 1-1   EMS Professionals

Dispatcher

A 9-1-1 call for help is usually received by an EMS dispatcher. This person is trained in obtaining information and determining what emergency personnel and equipment will likely be needed. The EMS dispatcher then sends the appropriate EMS unit to the scene.

First Responder

The first professional with BLS training to arrive at the scene of a medical emergency is called a first responder. This person may be you as a professional rescuer if you are close to the scene. The first responder generally takes over care of the victim from a lay person who may be giving first aid or from anyone with less training. The first responder also gathers any information concerning the victim, may control the scene or direct others to do so, and in some instances prepares for the arrival of an ambulance. In a healthcare setting a professional rescuer may provide emergency care until a physician, nurse, or other healthcare professional with a higher level of training takes over. In an out-of-hospital setting, emergency care may be given until emergency medical technicians arrive with an ambulance.

Emergency Medical Technician (EMT)

In an out-of-hospital emergency, EMTs usually arrive in an ambulance. They take over the medical care of the victim, give necessary medical care at the scene, and transport the victim for advanced medical care **(Figure 1-2)**. EMTs with

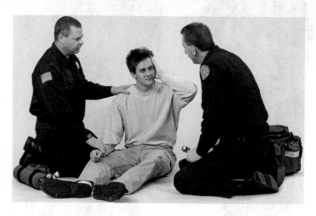

Figure 1-2 EMTs take over the prehospital care of a victim.

different levels of training perform different medical treatments. Paramedics are EMTs with the highest level of training.

Medical Director

The medical director is a physician within the EMS system who oversees the care given by EMTs and some first responders. The medical director establishes protocols for medical care to be given to victims at the scene and is available for consultation by radio or telephone to EMTs giving care.

Hospital Centers

First responders and EMTs provide prehospital care before and during the transport of the victim to a hospital. Depending on the medical care needed and facilities in the area, the victim receives care from physicians in a hospital emergency department or a specialized center such as a trauma center, burn center, or pediatric center.

job, and failing to care for a victim while you are on the job can make you legally liable.

State laws vary regarding your legal responsibility to act when off the job. Ask your instructor or research your state's laws to learn whether you are obligated to give care at an emergency you encounter as a private citizen.

Note, however, that even as a private citizen, once you begin to give care in an emergency, you have accepted and taken on an obligation to continue giving care. Abandoning a victim in this situation could lead to an injury or illness worsening, disability, or death for which you may be legally liable.

Consent

Before giving care, you must have the victim's **consent.** Touching another person without consent is a criminal action called battery. Consent may be either expressed or implied.

Expressed consent means the victim explicitly gives you permission for emergency care. Tell the victim who you are and that you have had basic life support training, and say what you want to do to help. The victim should understand that you are *asking* for consent, not stating what you plan to do regardless of what the victim wishes. A victim who is responsive (awake and alert) and able to communicate must give you expressed consent by telling you it is okay or by nodding agreement. With an injured or ill child, a parent or guardian who is present must give expressed consent.

If the victim is unresponsive, or a child's parent or guardian is not present and cannot be reached quickly enough for consent, then you have **implied consent** to give care in an emergency. You can assume, unless there is evidence to the contrary, that the person would, if able, consent to receiving care for a life-threatening condition.

Refusal of Consent

Most competent victims in a medical emergency will give consent when they understand the importance of the care you are offering. **Competent** means the person is able to understand what is happening and the implications of his or her decision. A victim may not be competent because of intoxication, the influence of a drug, or altered mental status caused by an injury or illness.

Rarely, a competent victim may refuse your care when you seek consent. The person may have religious reasons, may be afraid, may not trust you, or may have some other reason. Regardless of the reason, a competent adult has the right to refuse medical care, even care that has already begun, and you must not force care in this situation. The victim's refusal may be expressed through words, by shaking the head or signaling you to stop, or by trying to push you away. If this happens, follow these guidelines:

- Make sure 9-1-1 or advanced medical personnel have been called, even though the victim may seem to refuse all care. The victim might accept treatment from another medical professional.
- Keep talking to the victim, who may change his or her mind. Explain that you respect his or her right to refuse care but ask the person to reconsider. Explain what may happen if the victim does not receive care.
- To protect yourself legally, make sure someone else at the scene sees or hears the victim's refusal to accept your care, and document it as soon as you can.

Advance Directives

An advance directive is a specific form of refusing care. An **advance directive,** sometimes called a living will, is a legal document, signed by an individual, often a terminally ill person, and his or her doctor, that restricts what medical care the person will accept. Often this means the ill person has chosen not to be resuscitated if his or her heart and breathing stop. A written statement of this is called a **Do Not Resuscitate (DNR) order.** This would mean, for example, that the person does not want to receive CPR or defibrillation. Most terminally ill patients with DNR orders are in a hospital or nursing home, but some are at home. Because of the legal issues involved, a professional rescuer must be certain about the written DNR document before deciding not to give basic life support. Statements by a family member about what the victim would want, for example, cannot be used to withhold lifesaving care. A professional rescuer working in a healthcare facility where DNR orders are more common should follow the facility's policy for providing or withholding specific kinds of care. Note that a DNR order that refers to resuscitation does not apply to other kinds of treatment, which you should still provide.

Scope of Practice

As noted earlier, professional rescuers should give only the care they have been trained to give. The set of basic life support skills learned in this course, along with skills from other recognized courses, are part of your **scope of practice.** Acting outside your scope of practice, such as trying to do something you have seen others do but have not been trained to do yourself, may make you legally liable for the results of your actions.

Standard of Care

Standard of care refers generally to how you give care and what others with your same training would do in a similar situation. Standards are generally determined by professional organizations, laws, and other recognized authorities. You will learn the standards of care for basic life support in this course. Performing care in a way that does not meet the standards could result in the victim's injury or illness becoming worse, and you could be legally liable.

Negligence and Abandonment

Not following accepted standards of care when giving care is called **negligence.** In cases of negligence an injured party may sue to recover financial damages for the result of your actions. You may be found guilty of negligence only if three conditions are met:

1. You have a duty to act.
2. You breach that duty (by not acting or by acting incorrectly).
3. Your actions or inaction causes injury or damages (including such things as physical injury or pain).

Examples of negligent actions could include moving a victim unnecessarily, doing something you have not been trained to do, or failing to give care as you have been trained to.

   Abandonment is a specific type of negligence. Once you begin giving emergency care, you must not stop until another professional with equal or greater training takes over. If you leave the victim and the injury or illness becomes worse, you may be found guilty of abandonment. Note that abandonment is different from justified instances of stopping care, such as if you are exhausted and unable to continue or you are in imminent danger because of hazards at the scene.

Confidentiality

While giving care you may learn private information about the victim, and you should not share that information with anyone other than healthcare professionals caring for the victim. Although state laws vary in terms of precise definitions regarding violation of privacy, **confidentiality** is the general principle that you should not give out any private information about a victim to anyone except for those caring for the victim.

Documentation

In most cases, your employer requires that you document actions you take in an emergency. Most agencies and facilities use specific forms that you must complete shortly after giving emergency care. Be aware that any written record may become legal evidence, and document the incident fully and in factual detail. Sign and date this document and, when appropriate, include the names or signatures of witnesses.

Good Samaritan Laws

Most states have **Good Samaritan laws** designed to encourage people to help others in an emergency without worrying about being sued. These laws vary from state to state, but in general they are designed to protect people who give care in an emergency. Ask your instructor about your state's specific Good Samaritan law, which may have provisions about providing emergency care on or off the job.

   Good Samaritan laws do not provide blanket protection, however. You are legally protected only when you follow standards of care, obtain consent, and meet the other legal criteria previously described.

PREVENTING EMERGENCIES

Professional rescuers are often in a position to help prevent emergencies in the settings in which they work. Because most injuries can be prevented, they commonly occur when someone fails to prevent them by not following accepted safety standards or using common sense. It is beyond the scope of this book to cover the specific steps that can be taken to prevent injuries in all settings, but professional rescuers with a little research and observation can learn what the risks are in their own work settings and how to help others prevent injuries and other emergencies. Following are some general guidelines for injury prevention:

- In your workplace and home, take steps to prevent fires, accidental poisonings, and other injuries. Look for hazards and correct them.
- In the workplace, always follow safety procedures required by the Occupational Safety and Health Administration (OSHA). If you have received safety training, use it. It takes only one lapse from a safety procedure to lose a life.
- Use common sense when driving or engaging in activities involving injury risks. As Table 1-1 shows, the majority of injuries seen in hospital emergency departments result from motor vehicle crashes, falls, or being struck by or against an object or cut or pierced by an object.

   Like injuries, many sudden illness emergencies also can be prevented. A healthy lifestyle helps prevent heart attack, stroke, hypertension, diabetes, and other diseases that may result in life-threatening medical emergencies. A healthy lifestyle begins with avoiding the well-known risk factors that contribute to these diseases: stop smoking, eat a diet low in fats and sugars, exercise regularly, control your weight, and learn to manage stress. Chapter 5 describes these strategies for healthful living in more detail.

COPING WITH THE STRESS OF EMERGENCIES

Emergencies are stressful, especially when the victim does not survive. Not every victim can be saved. Injuries, illness, or circumstances are often beyond our control. Particularly stressful emergencies include those that involve multiple victims, children, victims of abuse or neglect, or death or injury of a co-worker or friend.

It is normal to have a strong emotional reaction during and immediately after a stressful emergency. Often this reaction gradually diminishes with time, but in some cases the stress remains and problems may result. Stress can cause irritability when interacting with others, difficulty sleeping, problems concentrating, general anxiety or depression, and even physical symptoms. If you recognize that you are feeling or behaving differently after experiencing a traumatic emergency, you may need help coping.

- Remind yourself that your reaction is normal, that we all need help sometimes.
- Talk to others: family members, co-workers, other professional rescuers, local emergency responders, or your own healthcare provider (without breaching confidentiality of the victim).
- Many organizations and facilities have a formal program involving a **critical incident stress debriefing,** which generally includes group discussions and the guidance of professionals trained in stress reduction. Do not hesitate to use such a program.
- Do not be afraid or reluctant to seek professional help. Many employers have an employee assistance program or member assistance program that can help or make a referral. Or ask your healthcare provider for a referral.

Conclusion

Professional rescuers work in a wide variety of settings but share the responsibility of giving emergency care, including basic life support, for injuries and sudden illness. Professional rescuers must clearly understand their responsibilities to be prepared for emergencies, their role within the EMS system, and the legal issues involved in giving care.

Case Scenario

Mark Johnson, a park ranger trained as a professional rescuer, encounters a lone hiker in a trail parking lot. The man is over 60 years of age and overweight. The man is leaning against his car, breathing fast, sweating heavily, one hand rubbing his chest. Mark stops to ask him if he is okay, and the man, short of breath and speaking with difficulty, says he is okay but too out of shape for the hike he just took. He grimaces as if in pain, and Mark asks if he is feeling chest pain. "It's just indigestion," the man says, and he waves Mark off when he offers help. Mark realizes, however, that the man could be having a heart attack.

1. Since the man has refused his offer to help, what should he do?
   a. Back away, but keep watching the man in case he collapses, in which case he has implied consent to give treatment.
   b. Nothing. He should now go on about his work, and later in the office write a report stating that the man refused care.
   c. Take the man's car keys away and call for an ambulance.
   d. Keep talking to the man and explain that he might be having a heart attack, which could become very serious if he ignores it; offer to call for help.

While Mark is talking to him, the man suddenly clutches his chest and collapses unresponsive. With his cell phone Mark calls 9-1-1 while positioning the man to assess his condition.

2. As a professional rescuer, what is Mark now legally obligated to do?
   a. Provide care as he has been trained to do.
   b. Respect the man's earlier refusal of care but stay with him until EMS personnel take over.
   c. Contact a family member for permission to care for him.
   d. Nothing—he has no legal obligations in this situation.

Preventing Infectious Disease

When caring for a victim in any emergency situation, there is some risk of transmission of infectious disease. That risk is very low, however, and taking steps to prevent being infected greatly reduces that risk.

HOW INFECTIOUS DISEASES ARE TRANSMITTED

The transmission of infectious disease occurs through a process involving four stages **(Figure 2-1)**:

1. *The process begins with the person (or other carrier) with the infection.*

2. *The infectious pathogen (disease-causing bacteria, virus, fungus, or parasite) leaves the infected person's body.* For example:
   - The person may bleed from a cut, and in that blood is the pathogen.
   - The person may sneeze out little droplets carrying the pathogen.

3. *The infectious pathogen reaches another person and enters his or her body.* This can happen in a number of ways:
   - The person may come into contact with the infected person's blood, other body fluid, or infectious material in a way that the pathogen enters his or her body through mucous membranes or nonintact skin (**bloodborne transmission**).
   - The person may inhale the pathogen in tiny droplets in the air (**airborne transmission**).
   - The person may be bitten by an insect, such as a tick or mosquito, carrying the pathogen (**vector transmission** of bloodborne pathogen).

   Transmission of a pathogen from one person to another is said to occur through direct or indirect contact:
   - **Direct contact** is contact with an infected person or fluids or substances from that person.
   - **Indirect contact** is contact with contaminated objects, food or drink, droplets in the air, or vectors such as insects.

4. *The second person develops the infection.* Just having the pathogen enter the body does not automatically mean a person will become ill. He or she may have been vaccinated against the disease, which means the body will kill the pathogen before it can cause disease. A person's natural immune system may also be able to kill some pathogens and thereby prevent illness. Or the person may become infected. The process then starts all over again.

THE OSHA BLOODBORNE STANDARD

Pathogens that can be transmitted through contact with an infected person's blood or other body fluids are called bloodborne pathogens. Because several of these diseases are very serious, the U.S. Occupational Safety and Health Administration (OSHA) has created safety standards for those who are likely in their work to encounter the body fluids of others, including many professional rescuers. The **Occupational Exposure to Bloodborne Pathogens Standard** (the Standard) was designed to eliminate or minimize employees' exposure to human blood and other potentially infectious materials (OPIM). The Standard applies to all employees who, as part of their job, may reasonably expect to be exposed to blood and OPIM that may contain pathogens. The Standard applies to employees who may be at risk even if their job for the most part does not involve giving emergency care or working near or with bloodborne pathogens **(Figure 2-2)**.

Figure 2-1 Different modes of disease transmission.

BLOODBORNE PATHOGENS

The U.S. Centers for Disease Control and Prevention (CDC) also provides guidelines for preventing exposure to bloodborne pathogens. Practices and procedures from both the CDC and OSHA are included in this chapter. Practices described here are also consistent with the standards of the National Fire Protection Association (NFPA) for infection control. Additional recommendations for infection control programs for fire departments can be found in NFPA 1581 (www.nfpa.org).

BLOODBORNE PATHOGENS

Several serious diseases can be transmitted from one person to another through contact with the infected person's blood. Bacteria or viruses that cause such diseases are also present in some other body fluids, such as semen, vaginal secretions, and bloody saliva or vomit. Other body fluids such as nasal secretions, sweat, tears, and urine do not usually transmit pathogens. Three serious bloodborne infections are HIV, hepatitis B, and hepatitis C.

HIV

Acquired immunodeficiency syndrome (AIDS) is caused by the **human immunodeficiency virus (HIV).** People with AIDS are more susceptible to certain infections, which invade the body as the disease progresses. The disease is eventually fatal.

Figure 2-2 The OSHA Bloodborne Standard protects employees in many different occupations.

The greatest risk involves exposure to the almost one million HIV-positive people in the United States, one-fourth of whom are unaware of their infection. The only reliable way to determine if a person has HIV is through a blood test. HIV is transmitted through an infected person's body fluids, including:

- Blood
- Semen
- Vaginal secretions
- Breast milk
- Other body fluids if blood is present in them

Although HIV can sometimes be detected in saliva, tears, urine, and other body fluids, exposure to these fluids from an infected person does not result in transmission of the virus. Casual contact with those infected with HIV also does not result in transmission of the virus. Casual contact includes sharing a meal or a drinking glass, touching, being around someone who sneezes or coughs, or sharing a phone or bathroom.

No vaccine is currently available for HIV, and there is no cure for AIDS. Therefore, preventive measures are very important. Safe care practices significantly reduce the risk of contracting HIV or

other infectious diseases. These guidelines include the following:

- Regular handwashing
- Use of barriers
- Standard precautions

These guidelines are discussed in detail later in this chapter.

Hepatitis B

Hepatitis B, also called serum hepatitis, is caused by the hepatitis B virus (HBV). HBV is transmitted by blood and materials contaminated with blood or body fluids. HBV infections are a major cause of liver damage, cirrhosis, and liver cancer. Because of routine hepatitis B vaccinations, the number of new infections per year has declined, but the CDC reports that HBV still infects about 80,000 people in the United States yearly, and there are about 1.25 million chronic carriers. About 5,000 people die every year of liver problems associated with HBV infection.

The most common mode of HBV transmission is direct contact with infectious blood. Exposure to HBV on contaminated environmental surfaces is another common mode of transmission. At room temperature the virus may survive for several days in dried body fluids on surfaces such as tables and faucets. HBV is easily transmitted because it can live longer outside the body and because very little blood is needed to cause infection. HBV can also be spread by sharing such personal items as a razor, toothbrush, or drug paraphernalia like needles and syringes. HBV is not transmitted in food or water, in fecal matter, through the air, or through casual contact.

A vaccine is available for HBV. Individuals who are more likely to come in contact with HBV-infected people, such as healthcare workers and professional rescuers, often get this vaccine. The law requires that employees who are at risk for HBV be offered free vaccinations by their employer. Those who have not been vaccinated can prevent infection by protecting themselves against exposure to blood. These include the same protections you should take to avoid all bloodborne pathogens.

Hepatitis C

Hepatitis C is a liver disease caused by the hepatitis C virus (HCV). This virus lives in the blood of people with the disease and is spread via the blood. The CDC reports that an estimated

2.7 million people in the United States have chronic HCV infection, and about 25,000 new infections occur each year. HCV does not always cause serious health problems. Many people who carry HCV have some liver damage but do not feel sick from it. In others, cirrhosis of the liver may develop, resulting in eventual liver failure.

In the general population, HCV spreads most often through drug injections with contaminated needles. For those employed in healthcare facilities, the primary risk of HCV transmission is via direct contact with infectious blood through an accidental needlestick or injury with other sharp objects. Blood tests can be done to determine if a person has HCV. The CDC recommends HCV testing for healthcare workers and professional rescuers who have been exposed to HCV-positive blood.

There currently is no vaccine available for HCV and no cure. Therefore, preventive measures are very important.

Airborne Pathogens

Two important airborne diseases are tuberculosis and meningitis.

Tuberculosis

Tuberculosis (TB) is transmitted through the air, typically when an infected person coughs or sneezes. TB made a comeback in the 1980s and 1990s, and although it is now declining again, about 16,000 cases are reported each year. Some forms of the tuberculosis bacteria have become resistant to treatment. Healthcare workers generally use precautions when caring for people known or suspected to have TB, but rarely does a professional rescuer need to take special precautions against airborne disease. Those employed in facilities where TB patients are treated should follow facility policies to prevent transmission.

Meningitis

Meningitis is a viral or bacterial infection of the fluid surrounding the spinal cord and brain. The bacterial forms are particularly serious; they are fatal in over 10% of the 3,000 cases that occur each year. The disease is spread through air droplets when an infected person coughs or sneezes, and through direct contact such as kissing or sharing utensils or drinking glasses. Children and adolescents have the highest incidence of meningitis, which is more common among those in crowded living conditions such as college students in dormitories.

A new vaccine against certain forms of meningitis was approved in 2005, and the CDC now recommends routine vaccination for preteens and those entering high school or college. Special precautions are unnecessary for professional rescuers except when caring for a victim or patient known to be infected.

Preventing Bloodborne Disease Transmission

The OSHA Standard requires that all employees who perform tasks involving potential occupational exposure to bloodborne pathogens receive annual training. This training should cover the hazards they face (how bloodborne diseases are transmitted and their symptoms), the protective measures they can take to prevent exposure, and procedures to follow if they are exposed.

The Standard requires use of four types of strategies to reduce exposure to bloodborne pathogens and prevent disease transmission:

1. Engineering controls
2. Work practice controls
3. Personal protection equipment
4. Standard precautions

All professional rescuers can use many of the same strategies to prevent infection.

Engineering Controls

Engineering controls are devices that isolate or remove the bloodborne pathogen hazard. These devices are commonly used in healthcare facilities and include needleless systems, eye wash stations, handwashing facilities, and biohazard labels.

Sharps is a general term for any devices or items that may accidentally cut a person handling them. Examples of sharps are needles, scissors, scalpels, and broken glassware. Approved sharps containers must also be available in appropriate places for safe disposal of used sharps **(Figure 2-3)**.

When appropriate, handwashing facilities must be provided for all employees. When not possible, antiseptic hand cleanser may be used instead. When using antiseptic towelettes or antibacterial handwashing liquid to wash your hands after being exposed to a victim's blood or body fluids, you still need to thoroughly scrub with soap and water as soon as possible.

Warning labels are required to be prominently displayed on any containers for wastes, blood, contaminated equipment or clothing, and other potentially infectious materials.

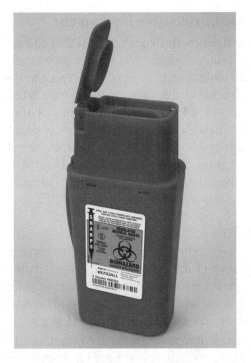

Figure 2-3 A sharps container.

Figure 2-4 Handwashing is an effective means of helping prevent disease transmission.

Work Practice Controls

Work practice controls reduce the likelihood of exposure by ensuring that tasks are performed in a safe manner. Work practice controls include using personal protection equipment (PPE), handwashing, decontamination and sterilization of equipment and areas, and good personal habits. Those employed in healthcare settings should also learn how to safely handle sharps, correctly dispose of wastes, and safely handle contaminated laundry, and other work practice controls.

Handwashing

Handwashing is a simple but very important step for preventing the transmission of bloodborne pathogens. Following are general guidelines for handwashing:

- Wash any exposed skin, ideally with antibacterial soap, as soon after an exposure as possible.
- While washing, be gentle with any scabs or sores.
- Wash all surfaces, including the backs of hands, wrists, between the fingers, and under fingernails **(Figure 2-4)**.
- Wash hands before and immediately after removing gloves or other personal protective equipment.

For handwashing after caring for a victim, you can use facilities such as restrooms, janitor closets, and laboratory sinks, as long as soap is available, but do not use sinks in areas where food is prepared. Remember to scrub thoroughly using soap—merely wetting the hands will not prevent infection.

Antiseptic towelettes and antibacterial handwashing liquid can be used when soap and running water are not available. When used for the initial cleaning after being exposed to a victim's blood or body fluids, however, a thorough scrubbing with soap and water is still needed as soon as possible **(Figure 2-5)**.

Decontamination and Sterilization

After providing emergency care involving a victim's body fluids, you may need to decontaminate or

Figure 2-5 Waterless antibacterial handwashing liquid and towelette.

sterilize the area or equipment. **Decontamination** is the use of physical or chemical means to remove, inactivate, or destroy bloodborne pathogens on a surface or item so that it is no longer infectious. To **sterilize** something means to use a chemical or physical procedure to destroy all microbial life on the item. Follow these general guidelines for decontamination and sterilization:

- All reusable sharps, such as knives, scissors, and scalpels, must be cleaned and sterilized after being used.
- Decontaminate equipment and working surfaces, bench tops, and floors with an approved disinfectant, such as a 10% bleach solution **(Figure 2-6)**.
- Disinfect personal items, such as jewelry, and nail brushes after handwashing.
- Use utensils, such as tongs or a dustpan, to clean up broken glass and other contaminated materials for disposal in a biohazard container.

Personal Habits

While and after caring for a victim when you may be exposed to bloodborne pathogens, prevent entry of pathogens into your mouth or eyes by keeping your hands away from your face. In general, follow these guidelines:

- Do not smoke.
- Do not put on lip balm, hand lotion, or cosmetics.
- Do not eat or drink.
- Do not handle your contact lenses.
- Do not use a sink that is used for food preparation for any other cleanup.

Personal Protective Equipment

Personal protective equipment (PPE) consists of barriers such as gloves and resuscitation masks that you use when caring for a victim in an emergency. In healthcare settings you may also have access to other forms of PPE, such as jumpsuits or aprons, face shields or face masks, eye shields or goggles, and caps and booties, that you wear to protect yourself from exposure to blood and OPIM.

In any situation where exposure to bloodborne pathogens is a possibility, wear your PPE.

Gloves

Gloves are a type of barrier. Like other barriers, they separate you from potentially infectious materials. When possible, wear gloves whenever providing care, not just when blood or other body fluids are obviously present. Follow these guidelines:

- ***Check that your gloves are intact.*** If a hole or tear is present, replace the glove immediately with a new one.
- ***Do not use petroleum-based hand lotions.*** These lotions may cause latex gloves to disintegrate.
- ***Remove contaminated gloves carefully.*** Do not touch any part of the contaminated outside of the gloves as you remove them **(Figure 2-7)**.
- ***Dispose of gloves properly.*** After touching any material that may be infected by bloodborne pathogens, dispose of your gloves in a container safe for biohazardous waste.

Resuscitation Masks

Resuscitation masks and other types of barriers provide protection when giving a victim rescue breathing or CPR. These are described fully in Chapter 4.

Improvising Personal Protection Equipment

In unexpected circumstances you may not have gloves or other PPE with you when potentially

Figure 2-6 Disinfect an area after a spill of blood or other potentially infectious material.

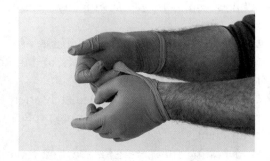

Figure 2-7 Removing contaminated glove.

Glove Latex Allergy

People who frequently wear latex gloves have a potential risk of developing a latex allergy. This reaction might include a skin rash or might even cause breathing difficulty. If you experience signs of an allergy when wearing gloves, ask your employer for latex-free or hypoallergenic gloves made of nitrile or vinyl.

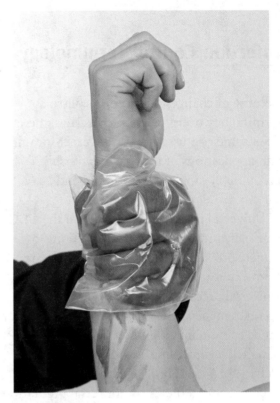

Figure 2-8 Always use a protective barrier, and improvise when necessary.

exposed to bloodborne pathogens in an emergency. Be creative in using items at hand to avoid contact with potentially infectious material. Using a plastic bag, a sheet, or a towel, or even removing an article of clothing to use as a barrier is better than being unprotected **(Figure 2-8)**. Dispose of or decontaminate any articles you use as barriers as you would any contaminated item.

Standard Precautions

Standard precautions, formerly called universal precautions, involve using safety guidelines in all caregiving situations and treating all blood and OPIM as if known to be contaminated. In most emergency situations you cannot readily identify precisely a body fluid present in order to evaluate whether it may or may not be infectious; therefore, OSHA recommends using standard precautions with *every* body fluid. Following standard precautions means using PPE and following all the safety guidelines previously described and learned in bloodborne pathogen training.

IF AN EXPOSURE OCCURS

Even when you follow all safety guidelines and standard precautions, when you give care in an emergency you can be unexpectedly exposed to pathogens. If you have been exposed, you need to take immediate action:

- If blood or OPIM splashes in your eyes or onto other mucous membranes, flush the area with running water for 20 minutes if possible.
- Immediately wash any exposed area well with soap, using an antibacterial soap if possible.
- Treat any scabs and sores gently when cleaning your skin.
- Report the exposure to your supervisor as soon as possible.
- Save any potentially contaminated object for testing purposes.
- Seek medical care as soon as possible.

OSHA requires employers to inform you how to make an incident report if you are exposed. After receiving your report, your employer must take additional steps to assist you in receiving any needed tests and medical treatment.

Exposure Control Plans

OSHA also requires employers of certain professional rescuers to have an **Exposure Control Plan** to prevent exposure to bloodborne pathogens. The employer's Exposure Control Plan should do the following:

- Identify the job positions and individuals to receive training
- Establish necessary engineering controls and work practice controls
- Specify PPE to be used
- Require the use of standard precautions
- State the opportunity for hepatitis B vaccination
- Include other measures appropriate for your specific work environment

Infection Control Terminology

Because of changes in infection control terminology over the last two decades, there has been some confusion about the exact meanings and applications of the terms *universal precautions, standard precautions,* and *body substance isolation.*

Universal precautions is the term the CDC originally promoted in 1987 for actions to protect providers of first aid and healthcare from exposure to bloodborne pathogens. Universal precautions apply to all people's blood, semen, vaginal secretions, and other body fluids containing visible blood, or to any objects potentially contaminated with any of these. In its 1991 Bloodborne Pathogens Standard, OSHA required the use of universal precautions, which it defined as "an approach to infection control. According to the concept of Universal Precautions, all human blood and certain human body fluids are treated as if known to be infectious for HIV, HBV, and other bloodborne pathogens." Many healthcare and first aid providers continue to use the term *universal precautions,* in part because it is the term used in federal laws and many state laws.

At the same time, many healthcare institutions were following principles of **body substance isolation (BSI),** an infection control concept that originated in efforts to control all infections (not just bloodborne pathogens) occurring within healthcare facilities. BSI precautions assume that *any* body fluid or moist body tissue is potentially infectious.

In 1996 the CDC published new guidelines called **standard precautions** intended primarily for infectious disease control within healthcare facilities. Standard precautions combine the major features of universal precautions and BSI precautions. Although some providers feel that standard precautions have replaced universal precautions, the CDC states: "Standard precautions were developed for use in hospitals and may not necessarily be indicated in other settings where universal precautions are used, such as child care settings and schools" (http://www.cdc.gov/ncidod/hip/Blood/UNIVERSA.HTM).

Because standard precautions are more rigorous than universal precautions, this text will use the term *standard precautions.* Recognize, however, that in many situations universal precautions are appropriate.

DISEASE PRECAUTIONS DURING BLS TRAINING

Learning and practicing basic life support skills involves working with manikins and other equipment. The risk of infectious disease transmission resulting from using this equipment is extremely low, and there have been no known cases of any significant disease transmission during BLS courses.

Nonetheless, because there is some risk, steps should be taken to prevent possible exposure to disease pathogens. Follow these guidelines:

- Tell your course instructor if you know you have any infectious disease, and follow the instructions given you.

- Wash your hands before handling equipment and before all class practice sessions.

- Follow instructions for how to handle manikins and all equipment.

- Clean manikins and other equipment that may harbor pathogens between all uses, following your instructor's directions for using a disinfecting or sterilizing solution such a bleach solution.

- Follow the manikin manufacturer's instructions for where and how to clean the manikin. Since commercial manikin models from different manufacturers may differ in the cleaning instructions, use only the directions supplied for the particular model you are using.

Following these general guidelines along with specific instructions from your instructor will help ensure a minimal risk of disease transmission for all participants in the course.

Conclusion

It is unlikely that a serious infectious bloodborne disease such as AIDS or hepatitis will be transmitted while giving basic life support in an emergency. The risk of such diseases for professional rescuers can be all but eliminated by using personal equipment such as gloves and other barriers and following standard precautions. If you are employed in a setting in which exposure to bloodborne pathogens is likely, you will receive OSHA-mandated training for additional steps to prevent disease transmission.

Case Scenario

You are called to a scene where, you are told, a woman collapsed in the employee parking lot after getting out of her car. She is unresponsive when you arrive. When she fell in the gravel, she apparently struck her face, which now has some blood on it. You position her on her back and quickly determine that she is not breathing and has no pulse.

1. Before starting CPR, you should
   a. check with the personnel office to see if the woman's file indicates she has an infectious disease.

   b. wipe her face clean with a disinfecting solution.

   c. put on gloves.

   d. return to your vehicle to get protective coveralls and a face shield.

Another employee calls for additional help while you put on gloves and start basic life support. Within a few minutes you have successfully resuscitated the woman, and the ambulance arrives. After the victim is transported, you clean up the scene.

2. When you remove your gloves, you notice a small tear in one of them and a substance that may be blood on your hand. What should you do *first?*
   a. Call your employer to report the possible exposure.

   b. Wash your hands thoroughly with soap and running water.

   c. Quickly drive home and soak your hand in a solution of bleach in water.

   d. Call your physician to check your immunization records.

Chapter 3

Victim Assessment and Basic Life Support

Basic life support skills are used to resuscitate a victim who is not breathing adequately or does not have a heartbeat, or to keep the victim alive until advanced medical care is available. Care of the victim begins with the initial assessment of the victim's airway, breathing, and circulation: the **ABCs.**

OVERVIEW OF BASIC LIFE SUPPORT

Of all injuries and illnesses, the most immediate threats to life are those involving the airway, breathing, or circulation of blood. When a problem occurs in any of these areas, the victim's body cells do not receive enough oxygen. Brain cells begin to die within minutes. The victim needs immediate basic life support to survive. The goals of basic life support are to:

- Resuscitate the victim if possible by restoring an open airway and adequate breathing and circulation.
- Ensure that the victim receives advanced medical care (call for help).
- Keep the victim alive until he or she receives advanced medical care.
- Prevent the victim's condition from getting worse.

Basic life support generally consists of three general categories of care, often collectively called **resuscitation.** First, a victim who is not breathing needs rescue breathing to move oxygen into the body to keep body cells alive. Second, a victim whose heart is not beating also needs the chest compressions of CPR to circulate the blood so that oxygen reaches vital organs. If the victim is not breathing adequately because of an airway obstruction, or choking, this victim also needs care to clear the airway to allow either natural breathing or rescue breathing. Finally, a victim whose heart may be in a condition called ventricular fibrillation, which is common after heart attacks and other situations, may benefit from an electrical shock

given by an automated external defibrillator (AED) to restore a regular heartbeat.

The next four chapters describe these dimensions of basic life support in detail. This chapter discusses how to begin the process of basic life support by assessing the victim to detect these immediate threats to life.

Differences Among Adults, Children, and Infants

Because of size and other differences, there are some distinctions in how BLS skills are used with adults, children, and infants. These age-dependent differences result from anatomical and physiological differences in the human body at different ages. Differences in BLS techniques are described throughout the next four BLS chapters. Standard age groups for BLS are defined in the following way. Remember these age categories in reference to all BLS techniques:

- An *infant* is up to 1 year of age.
- A *child* for purposes of all BLS skills (including rescue breathing and CPR) is 1 year up to the onset of adolescence or puberty (as determined by the occurrence of secondary sex characteristics, such as the presence of armpit hair in boys or breast development in girls); for AED only, a child means ages 1 to 8.
- An *adult* for all BLS skills except for AED means at or past puberty; for AED only, adult means over age 8.

THE CARDIAC CHAIN OF SURVIVAL

Although BLS includes care given to any victim whose breathing or circulation stops, cardiac arrest

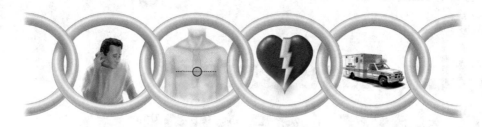

Figure 3-1 Cardiac chain of survival.

victims are a common type of victim needing BLS. **Cardiac arrest** refers to a sudden stop in the beating of the heart.

To recognize the urgent need for quick actions to save the lives of cardiac arrest victims, the Citizen CPR Foundation created the concept of the cardiac **chain of survival (Figure 3-1)**. This chain has four crucial links:

1. *Early Recognition and Access.* Recognize that a victim whose heart has stopped *needs help immediately!* It is also important that you recognize the signs and symptoms of a potential life-threatening condition such as a heart attack or a stroke in a responsive person (see Chapter 5). Do not wait until a person becomes unresponsive to start the chain of events needed to keep him or her alive. Call 9-1-1 and get help on the way. The victim needs early access to advanced medical care.

2. *Early CPR.* For a victim without a pulse, start cardiopulmonary resuscitation (CPR) immediately. This helps keep the brain and other vital organs supplied with oxygen until the AED arrives.

3. *Early Defibrillation.* An AED, usually present in healthcare agencies as well as in many public and work places, can help get the heart beating normally again after a cardiac arrest. Send someone right away to get the AED.

4. *Early Advanced Care.* The sooner the victim is treated by advanced emergency care professionals, the better the chance for survival. You can help make sure the victim reaches this last link in the chain by acting immediately with the earlier links.

CALL FIRST/CALL FAST

In any situation in which you recognize that a victim of injury or illness is unresponsive, if someone else is present at the scene, have that person call for help immediately. Shout for anyone who may hear you, and have them get help or call 9-1-1 and go for an AED.

If you are alone, however, you need to decide whether to call immediately or to first begin to provide care for the victim. The following guidelines are based on determinations of what is usually needed for victims in different circumstances.

As a general rule, if you are alone with an adult victim you should **call first** for help and an AED before providing CPR. For a child victim, **call fast** after providing about 5 cycles of CPR (about 2 minutes).

The rescue response should depend on the most likely cause of the victim's problem. **Call first** for a victim *of any age seen to collapse suddenly.* These victims are more likely to have a dysrhythmia and to require defibrillation. Calling EMS immediately starts the process of getting an AED to the victim sooner.

For unresponsive victims in cardiac arrest because of a likely asphyxial arrest, such as a downing victim or a child likely to have an airway obstruction, **call fast.** Give about 5 cycles of CPR (about 2 minutes) before stopping to call EMS.

THE INITIAL ASSESSMENT

When you recognize that an emergency is occurring, first check that it is safe to approach the victim, and then quickly assess the victim for immediate threats to life.

Scene Safety

In many emergency situations, hazards may be present in the scene that threaten your own safety. Always check the scene before approaching a victim: you must be safe yourself if you are to help another. Look for hazards such as smoke or flames, spilled chemicals or fumes, downed electrical wires, traffic dangers, and so on. If the scene is dangerous and you cannot safely approach the victim, *stay away and call for help.* The 9-1-1 dispatcher will send a crew with the appropriate training and equipment to safely reach and care for the victim.

Positioning the Victim

When you first reach the victim, quickly check him or her in the position found. Spinal and other injuries could be made worse by moving the victim unnecessarily. Tap the victim on the shoulder and ask "Are you okay?" A victim who can speak, cough, or make other sounds is breathing and has a heartbeat, and you may not need to move the victim. If the victim is unresponsive, try to determine whether the airway is open by looking, listening, and feeling for breathing through the nose or mouth without moving the victim. Put your ear close to the victim's mouth and listen and feel for breaths while watching the chest for the rise and fall of breathing.

If the victim is not breathing, or you cannot tell, then you need to position the victim on his or her back so that you can open his or her airway and check for adequate breathing. If the victim sustained trauma, however, he or she may have a spinal injury, requiring special precautions.

Precautions with Spinal Injuries

To position an unresponsive victim with a potential spinal injury, support the head in line with the body as you move the victim. This usually requires the help of others. If the victim is lying face down, with the help of one or two others, roll the victim onto his or her back, supporting the head through the whole move (**Figure 3-2**).

Checking the ABCs

The assessment begins by checking the victim for responsiveness. A victim who does not respond to your touch and voice, and who is not obviously conscious and awake, is unresponsive. Shout or have someone call for help as you move to the next step: checking the airway, breathing, and circulation (the **ABCs**). Always check in this order:

   A = Airway
   B = Breathing
   C = Circulation

If the victim can speak or cough, then he or she has an open airway, is breathing, and has a beating heart. This victim should then quickly be checked for life-threatening bleeding and other injuries.

Opening the Airway

The airway is the route by which air moves from the mouth and nose through the throat (pharynx) and into the lungs. The airway may be blocked by something stuck in the throat, by swollen airway tissues in a victim with a severe allergic reaction or a neck injury, or by an unresponsive victim's own tongue. The tongue can block the airway in an unresponsive victim lying on the back because of the weight of the tongue and relaxation of the muscles.

In an unresponsive victim, you need to ensure the airway is open. When the victim is lying face up, you must prevent the tongue from obstructing the airway by positioning the victim's head to open the airway. The technique used to open the airway depends on whether the victim may have a spinal injury.

In a victim not suspected of having a spinal injury, tilt the head back and lift the chin as shown in **Figure 3-3**. This is called the head tilt–chin

Figure 3-2 Positioning a victim with a potential spinal injury to assess the ABCs.

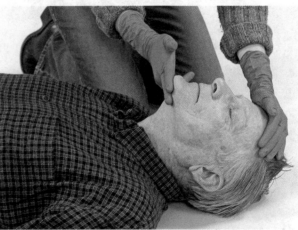

Figure 3-3 Head tilt–chin lift.

lift. This position moves the tongue away from the opening into the throat to allow air to pass through the airway **(Figure 3-4)**.

If the victim may have a spinal injury, do not tilt the head back to open the airway. Instead, only lift the jaw upward using both hands **(Figure 3-5)**. This is called a jaw thrust.

The maneuvers for checking the airway described before are used for an unresponsive victim. A responsive victim may have a blocked airway too, however, usually caused by choking on some object lodged in the throat. This victim will be unable to speak or make other sounds and typically signals the inability to breathe by clutching at the neck. A choking victim needs immediate care to clear the airway, as described in Chapter 6.

Checking Breathing

After opening the victim's airway, check immediately for adequate breathing **(Figure 3-6)**. Lean over with your ear close to the person's mouth and nose and *look* at the victim's chest to see if it rises

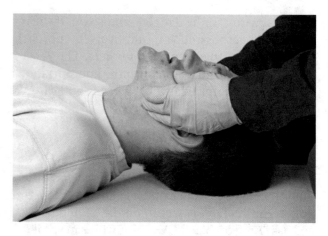

Figure 3-5 Jaw thrust.

and falls with breathing. *Listen* for any sounds of breathing, and *feel* for breath on your cheek. If the victim is breathing, put him or her in the recovery position (see the Skill: Recovery Position). If you do not detect any signs of breathing within 10 seconds, assume the person is not breathing adequately. Lack of adequate breathing may be caused by an obstructed airway (choking) or other causes.

At this point, give two breaths to a victim who is not breathing. Using a barrier device such as a resuscitation mask (see Chapter 4), or sealing your mouth over the victim's, blow air into the victim over 1 second. These breaths help determine whether the airway is open while also providing oxygen the body needs. Watch for a rise and fall in the victim's chest to ensure your breath is entering

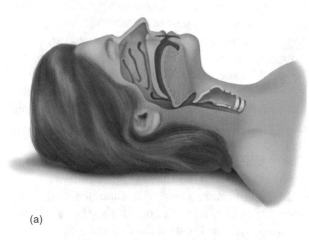

(a)

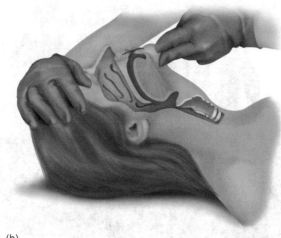

(b)

Figure 3-4 (a) In an unresponsive victim, the tongue may block the airway. (b) The head tilt–chin lift opens the airway.

Figure 3-6 Checking breathing.

the victim's lungs. If your first breath does not go in, attempt to reposition the victim with the head tilt–chin lift or jaw thrust to ensure the airway is open, and try again. If your next breath still does not go in, the victim is choking. Give care as described in Chapter 6.

The jaw thrust technique can be difficult to use, particularly when positioning a face mask. If you cannot successfully open the airway with the jaw thrust, however, then switch to the head tilt–chin lift method. It is more important to open the airway than to be overly concerned with a possible spinal injury.

Note that a victim who is found to be breathing may not be breathing *adequately.* As discussed in Chapter 4, a victim who is found not to be breathing adequately when the ABCs are checked is, like a victim who is not breathing at all, given rescue breaths.

Checking Circulation

Next check for circulation. This means checking that the heart is beating and blood is moving through the body (circulating). If the victim's heart has stopped or the victim is bleeding profusely, vital organs are not receiving enough oxygen to sustain life. **If the victim is moving, coughing, speaking, or breathing, his or her heart is beating.**

To check circulation, look first for obvious signs of circulation, such as signs of breathing, coughing, and movement. The surest sign of circulation is the presence of a **pulse (Figure 3-7)**. It takes training to be able to effectively and quickly locate a pulse. To check the pulse in an adult, use the **carotid pulse** in the neck. Holding the victim's forehead with one hand to keep the airway open, put the index and middle fingers of your other hand on the side of the victim's neck nearer you. Find the Adam's apple and then slide your fingertips toward you and down the victim's neck to the groove at the side of the neck. Pressing gently, feel for a pulse for at least 5 but not more than 10 seconds.

In a child, check either the carotid or the femoral pulse. The **femoral pulse** is located in the center of the groin crease.

To check the pulse in an infant, use the **brachial pulse** in the inside of the upper arm instead of the carotid pulse. With one hand on the infant's forehead to maintain head position for an open airway, put the fingers of your other hand about midway between the shoulder and elbow on the inside of the arm and press gently, feeling for no more than 10 seconds.

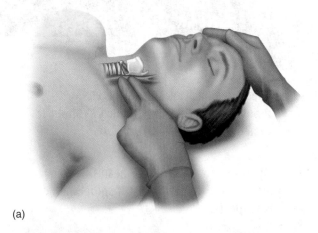

(a)

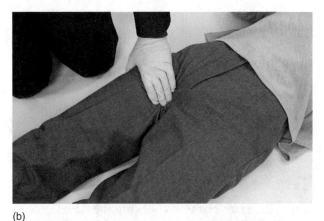

(b)

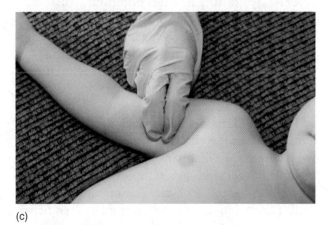

(c)

Fig 3-7 Checking the pulse. (a) Carotid pulse. (b) Femoral pulse. (c) Brachial pulse.

Lack of a definite pulse along with the absence of adequate breathing signifies the heart has stopped or is not beating effectively enough to circulate blood. If the victim lacks a pulse and is not breathing adequately, start cardiopulmonary resuscitation (CPR) and call for an automated external defibrillator (AED) to be brought to the scene, as described in Chapters 5 and 7. See the Skill: Check the ABCs.

Skill: Check the ABCs

1 Check responsiveness. Tap the victim's shoulder and ask "Are you okay?" Shout for someone to call 9-1-1.

2 Open the airway with the head tilt–chin lift, or with the jaw thrust if spinal injury is suspected.

3 Look, listen, and feel for breathing.

4 If the victim is not breathing adequately, give two rescue breaths. Seal the mask and keep the airway open. Watch the chest rise with each breath.

5 a. If breaths do not go in, reposition the head to open the airway again and give two breaths.
b. If breaths still do not go in, give care for obstructed airway.

6 Check circulation: look for severe bleeding and check the pulse. If no pulse, call for an AED and start CPR.

THE SECONDARY ASSESSMENT

If the initial assessment checking the ABCs reveals any life-threatening conditions, you immediately begin care for those conditions. Only if it is clear that the victim does not have a life-threatening condition, including bleeding, do you move on to the **secondary assessment** to check for additional injuries or signs of a sudden illness requiring care.

The secondary assessment includes obtaining a history from the victim or others present about what happened, what may have led to the illness or injury, other signs and symptoms, and so on. It may also include a physical examination of the victim to find injuries or other problems requiring care that are not immediately apparent. These skills are typically taught in first aid and first responder courses.

THE RECOVERY POSITION

An unresponsive victim who does not have a breathing or circulation problem, and who is not suspected to have a spinal injury, should be put in the **recovery position.** This position is used for several reasons:

- It helps keep the airway open so that you do not need to maintain the head tilt–chin lift position.
- It allows fluids to drain from the mouth so that the victim does not choke on blood, vomit, or other fluids.
- It prevents the victim from inhaling stomach contents if the victim vomits.

If possible, unless this could worsen the victim's injury, put the victim on his or her left side. Because of anatomical differences in the body, the left side has more benefits for protecting the victim. See the Skill: Recovery Position for the steps for moving an unresponsive breathing adult or child into the recovery position. The modified HAINES position is used to minimize movement of the head and neck in a victim with a potential spinal injury. **Figure 3-8** shows how to hold an infant in the recovery position.

Once the victim is in the recovery position, continue to monitor his or her breathing while waiting for advanced help to arrive.

Skill: **Recovery Position**

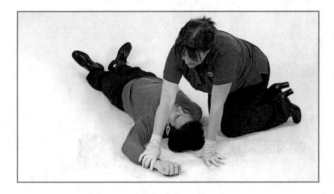

1 Extend the victim's arm that is farther from you above the victim's head.

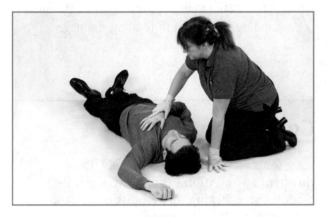

2 Position the victim's other arm across the chest.

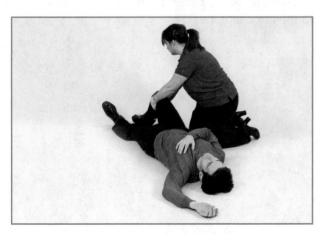

3 Bend the victim's nearer leg at the knee.

4 Put your forearm that is nearer the victim's head under the victim's nearer shoulder with your hand under the hollow of the neck.

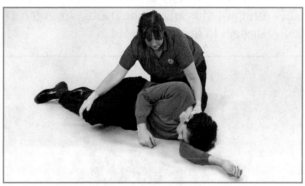

5 Carefully roll the victim away from you by pushing on the victim's flexed knee and lifting with your forearm while your hand stabilizes the head and neck. The victim's head is now supported on the raised arm.

(continued)

S k i l l : **Recovery Position** *(continued)*

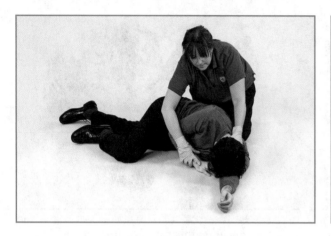

6   While continuing to support the head and neck, position the victim's hand palm-down with fingers under the armpit of the raised arm, with forearm flat on the surface at 90 degrees to the body.

7   With victim now in position, check the airway and open the mouth to allow drainage.

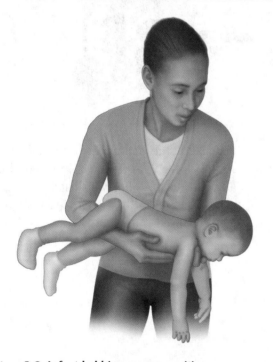

Figure 3-8 Infant held in recovery position.

Conclusion

Care for a victim with a potentially life-threatening condition begins with the initial assessment: checking for responsiveness and the victim's ABCs. Problems found with the airway, breathing, or circulation must be treated immediately. The basic life support skills used to care for these problems are described in the following chapters.

Case Scenario

You and your partner are called to a home where a caller says an elderly gentlemen is experiencing chest pains and other signs and symptoms that may indicate a heart attack. As you enter, you see the elderly gentleman stand up from his chair and then collapse on the floor onto his side. You begin your initial assessment and find that he is unresponsive. You roll him onto his back.

1. What action should you take *next?*
   a. Open his airway
   b. Check his breathing
   c. Take his pulse
   d. Move him into the recovery position

You use the head tilt–chin lift technique to open his airway. You put your ear close to his mouth and look, listen, and feel for breathing.

2. He is not breathing. Now what do you do?
   a. Take his pulse
   b. Use the jaw thrust to open his airway
   c. Give two rescue breaths
   d. Wait for your partner to set up the automated external defibrillator (AED) he has brought from the vehicle.

Keeping his airway open, you give two rescue breaths. Your breaths go in, and you observe his chest rising and falling. Your partner is still setting up the AED.

3. What is your *next* action?
   a. Continue rescue breathing
   b. Position him in the recovery position
   c. Wait for an AED to be ready to use
   d. Check his circulation

The victim does not have a pulse. Your partner is still setting up the AED.

4. What should you do until the AED is ready?
   a. Start CPR
   b. Position him for the AED and wait
   c. Put him in the recovery position
   d. Check him again for breathing

Chapter 4

Basic Life Support 1: Rescue Breathing

The most serious breathing emergency is respiratory arrest, in which breathing stops due to an injury or illness. When the initial assessment shows the victim is not breathing or not breathing adequately, it is crucial to act immediately because cells in vital organs begin to die within minutes.

RESPIRATORY EMERGENCIES

Any illness or injury that results in a victim no longer breathing, or breathing so ineffectively that the body is not receiving sufficient oxygen, is a respiratory emergency. The two primary types of breathing emergencies are respiratory arrest and respiratory distress. A respiratory emergency can result from many different causes, such as:

- A physical obstruction in the airway, such as food blocking the pharynx, or immersion in water
- An injury to the chest
- An illness affecting the lungs or airway, such as emphysema or asthma
- Heart problems
- An electrical shock
- A drug overdose or poisoning
- A severe allergic reaction

Regardless of the cause, body cells begin to die soon after losing their oxygen supply. Brain cells are very susceptible to low levels of oxygen and begin to die as soon as 4 minutes after oxygen is cut off. Within 6 minutes, brain damage is likely. Death is likely soon after.

Respiratory arrest means that breathing has completely stopped. With **respiratory distress,** the victim is still breathing, but the breathing may be difficult and becoming a serious problem. **Inadequate breathing** may also occur in an unresponsive victim who is breathing so slowly that oxygen levels in the blood are dropping to life-threatening levels.

RESPIRATORY DISTRESS

A victim in respiratory distress may be gasping for air, panting, breathing faster or slower than normal, or making wheezing or other sounds with breathing. Typically the victim cannot speak a full sentence without pausing to breathe. The victim's skin may look pale and be cool and moist; the lips and nail beds may be bluish. Lowered oxygen levels in the blood may make the victim feel dizzy or disoriented. The victim may be sitting and leaning forward, hands on knees, in what is called the **tripod position.**

Because respiratory distress in an infant or child may rapidly progress to arrest, it is crucial to act quickly when an infant or child has a problem breathing. In addition to the signs and symptoms described before, an infant or child may have flaring nostrils and more obvious movements of chest muscles with the effort to breathe.

Call for help immediately for any victim with sudden unexplained breathing problems. Help the victim rest in position of easiest breathing (often sitting up). Ask the victim about any prescribed medicine he or she may have, and help the victim take it if needed. For example, an asthmatic victim may need help using a **bronchodilator,** or a victim of an allergic reaction might need help with an emergency epinephrine kit such as an **EpiPen® (Figure 4-1)**. Stay with the victim and be prepared to give BLS if the victim becomes unresponsive. Administer supplemental oxygen to the victim if it is available and you are trained in its use (see Chapter 9).

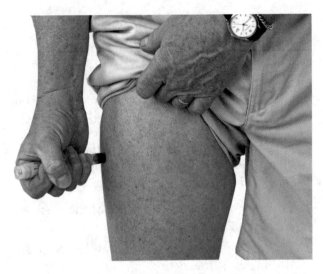

Figure 4-1 Position the EpiPen® firmly against the thigh to make the injection for anaphylaxis.

RESPIRATORY ARREST AND INADEQUATE BREATHING

Respiratory arrest and inadequate breathing are life-threatening emergencies. When you check the ABCs in a child or infant, look only for the presence or absence of breathing. In an adult, however, check for adequate breathing. If an adult victim is breathing at a rate less than 10 breaths per minute, take this as a sign of inadequate breathing—the victim is not receiving sufficient oxygen. In an adult who is not breathing adequately, do not wait for respiratory arrest before beginning to provide rescue breaths.

Rescue Breathing

Rescue breathing, once called mouth-to-mouth resuscitation, is a technique of blowing air or oxygen into a nonbreathing person's lungs to oxygenate the blood. If the victim's breathing has stopped but the heart is still beating, rescue breathing adds oxygen into the blood that is still circulating to vital tissues, keeping the victim alive until breathing starts again spontaneously or advanced care is given. If the victim also has no pulse, rescue breathing is combined with chest compressions in CPR to help circulate the oxygenated blood to vital organs (see Chapter 5).

Rescue breathing is given with the rescuer's own exhaled air unless special equipment is available. The air around us contains about 21% oxygen, and the breath we exhale is about 16% oxygen—still enough oxygen to increase the oxygen level in the victim's blood to maintain life.

Start rescue breathing immediately when you check the ABCs and discover the victim is not breathing. A victim in respiratory arrest may also be in cardiac arrest, so have someone call for help immediately. If an AED is available, send someone to get it (see Chapter 7).

Use of Barrier Devices

Barrier devices are always recommended when giving rescue breathing. Two common types of barrier devices are pocket masks and face shields **(Figure 4-2)**. Both devices offer protection from the victim's saliva and other fluids, as well as from the victim's exhaled air when the barrier is equipped with a one-way valve. With either device, keep the victim's head positioned to maintain an open airway as you deliver rescue breaths through the device.

Face Masks

The resuscitation mask, often called a pocket face mask or simply a face mask, seals over the victim's mouth and nose and has a port through which the rescuer blows air to give rescue breaths. A one-way valve allows the rescuer's air in through the mouthpiece, but the victim's exhaled air exits the mask through a different opening.

When using a face mask, it is essential to seal the mask well to the victim's face while maintaining an open airway. How you hold the mask depends on your position by the victim, whether the head tilt–chin lift or jaw thrust technique is used to open the airway, and whether you have one or two hands free to seal the mask. The following hand positions assume you have both hands free to seal the mask, whether alone at the victim's side while performing CPR or at the victim's head (alone giving only rescue breathing, or with another rescuer who is providing chest compressions).

Figure 4-2 Barrier devices.

From a position at the victim's side (when giving CPR) using the head tilt–chin lift:

1. With the thumb and index finger of your hand closer to the top of the victim's head, seal the top and sides of the mask to the victim's head as shown in **Figure 4-3a.**

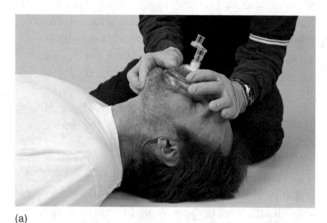

(a)

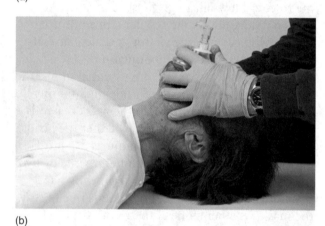

(b)

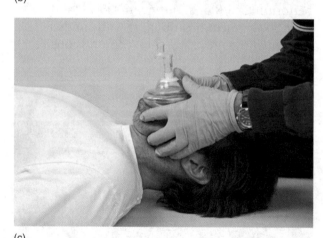

(c)

Figure 4-3 (a) Face-mask hand position with rescuer at victim's side. (b) Face-mask hand position with rescuer at victim's head using the head tilt–chin lift. (c) Face-mask hand position used with jaw thrust for a victim with spinal injury.

2. Put the thumb of your second hand on the lower edge of the mask.

3. Put the remaining fingers of your second hand under the jaw to lift the chin.

4. Press the mask down firmly to make a seal as you perform a head tilt–chin lift to open the airway.

From a position at the top of the victim's head (with two rescuers, or when not giving CPR) using the head tilt–chin lift:

1. Put your thumbs on both sides of the mask as shown in **Figure 4-3b.**

2. Put the remaining fingers of both hands under the angles of the victim's jaw on both sides.

3. As you tilt the head back, press the mask down firmly to make a seal as you lift the chin with your fingers.

From a position at the top of the victim's head using the jaw thrust:

1. Without tilting the victim's head back, position your thumbs on the mask the same as for the head tilt–chin lift from the top of the victim's head, with fingers under the angles of the jaw.

2. Lift the jaw to open the airway as you press down with your thumbs to seal the mask, without tilting the head back **(Figure 4-3c).**

Face Shield

Like a mask, a face shield is positioned over the victim's mouth as a protective barrier. The victim's nose, however, must be pinched closed when giving a rescue breath to prevent the air from coming out the nose instead of entering the lungs.

Bag Mask

Bag mask (BVM) units, like regular face masks, protect the rescuer from disease transmission, but they are also more effective for providing ventilations and give nonbreathing victims a greater concentration of oxygen. A professional rescuer alone can use the BVM, although it can be difficult for one person to maintain an open airway, seal the mask to the victim's face, and squeeze the bag. Two rescuers can usually be more effective in using the BVM. Chapter 9 describes this advanced skill.

If No Barrier Device Is Available

If no barrier device is available, give rescue breathing directly from your mouth to the victim's mouth, nose, or stoma if present. The risk of disease transmission is still very low.

Mouth to Mouth

Pinch the victim's nose shut and seal your mouth over the victim's mouth. Blow into the victim's mouth, watching the chest rise to confirm that the air is going in, and then remove your mouth to let the air escape.

Mouth to Nose

If the victim's mouth cannot be opened or is injured, or if you cannot get a good seal with your mouth over the victim's mouth, give rescue breathing through the nose. Hold the victim's mouth closed, seal your mouth over the nose to blow in, and then allow the mouth to open to let the air escape.

Mouth to Stoma

Because of past illness or injury, some people breathe through a hole in their lower neck called a **stoma.** During your check of the ABCs, check this hole to see if the victim is breathing. To give rescue breathing, cup your hand over the victim's nose and mouth to prevent your air from leaving by the nose and mouth instead of going to the lungs. Then seal your mouth or barrier device over the stoma, and give rescue breaths as usual.

Mouth to Nose and Mouth

Because of their smaller size, infants and very small children are generally given rescue breathing through both their mouth and nose. Seal your mouth over both the nose and mouth and give gentle breaths as usual, watching to see the chest rise with each breath.

Technique of Rescue Breathing

With the victim on his or her back, open the airway using the head tilt–chin lift, or the jaw thrust if the victim may have a spinal injury. Use a barrier device but do not delay rescue breathing to get one. The basic technique of rescue breathing is to blow air into the victim while watching the chest rise to make sure your air is going into the lungs. Do not try to rush the air in or blow too forcefully. Do not take a big breath in order to exhale more air into the victim; just take a normal breath as usual. Give each breath over about 1 second. If the breath does not go in, if you feel resistance or do not see the victim's chest rise, then try again to open the airway. If your breath still does not go in, then the

victim has an airway obstruction and needs care for choking (see Chapter 6). If your initial breath does go in, give a second breath over 1 second.

If the breaths go in, check for a pulse. If the victim has a pulse but is not breathing, continue rescue breathing as needed at a rate of one breath every 5 to 6 seconds in an adult or every 3 to 5 seconds for a child. The Skill: Rescue Breathing describes the sequence of steps in rescue breathing.

Rescue Breathing for Infants

Rescue breathing for infants is similar to that for adults and children, with these differences:

- Gently tilt the head back to open the airway and check breathing—do not overextend the neck.
- If no barrier device is available, cover both mouth and nose with your mouth to give breaths. (Use the mouth or nose only if you cannot cover both.)
- Give a breath every 3 to 5 seconds.

Cricoid Pressure

Cricoid pressure, also called the Sellick maneuver, is a technique that prevents the air given during rescue breathing from passing through the esophagus to the stomach. Air in the stomach can cause vomiting, which interrupts rescue breathing and carries the risk of **aspiration,** the movement of vomit or other fluids or solids into the lungs, which can cause a serious infection and other problems. Cricoid pressure put on the trachea squeezes the esophagus closed, preventing air from traveling to the stomach **(Figure 4-4).**

Cricoid pressure is performed only on unresponsive victims, only by a rescuer trained in this technique, and only by an additional rescuer who uses the technique while other rescuer(s) perform rescue breathing and CPR chest compressions if needed. Cricoid pressure can be used with an adult, child, or infant, using less pressure for smaller victims. Follow these steps:

1. With your index finger, locate the victim's Adam's apple (thyroid cartilage).

2. Slowly slide your finger down the victim's neck. Feel the indentation just past the bottom of the thyroid cartilage and, just below this, the higher cricoid cartilage.

3. With index finger and thumb, apply moderate pressure down on the cricoid cartilage. Maintain this pressure continuously while rescue breathing is being given.

Skill: Rescue Breathing

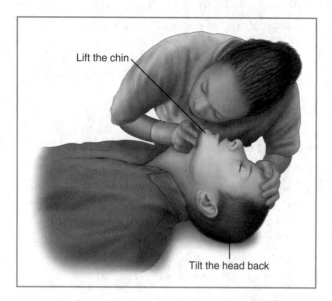

Lift the chin

Tilt the head back

1   Open the airway. Look, listen, and feel for adequate breathing for up to 10 seconds.

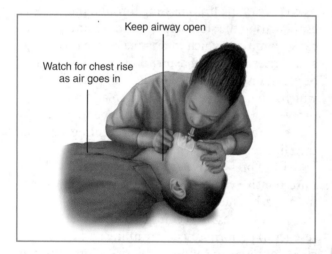

Keep airway open

Watch for chest rise as air goes in

2   If not breathing adequately, give 2 breaths over 1 second each, watching the chest rise and letting it fall.

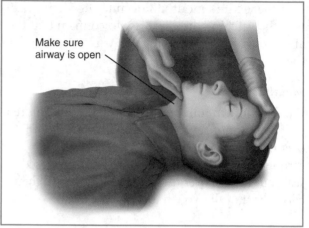

Make sure airway is open

3   If the first breath does not go in, try again to open the airway and give another rescue breath. If it still does not go in, the victim may be choking. Proceed to CPR for choking.

4   If your first 2 breaths go in, check the victim for no more than 10 seconds for a pulse. If there is a pulse but no adequate breathing, continue rescue breathing. Give each breath over 1 second, at rate of 10 to 12 breaths per minute (1 breath every 5–6 seconds) for an adult (or about 12 to 20 breaths per minute for an infant or child: 1 breath every 3–5 seconds), rechecking for a pulse about every 2 minutes. If there is no pulse, start CPR beginning with chest compressions.

ALERT

- Do not blow harder than is needed to make the chest rise.
- After each breath, remember to let the air escape and the chest fall.
- Blowing in too forcefully or for too long is ineffective and may put air in the stomach, which may cause vomiting.

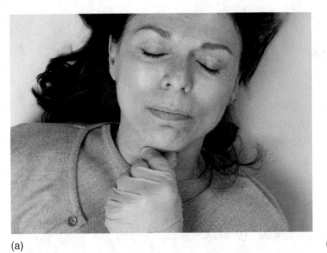

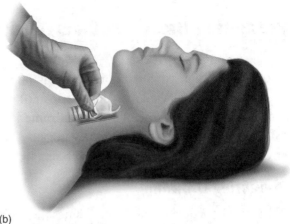

(a)   (b)

Figure 4-4 (a) The hand position for cricoid pressure. (b) Cricoid pressure compresses the esophagus against the spine.

Special Circumstances for Rescue Breathing

In some circumstances you may have to adjust how you give rescue breathing or respond to a changing situation. These circumstances include a victim vomiting, a victim wearing dentures, and a victim with facial injuries.

Vomiting

Usually, if the head is positioned correctly to open the airway and rescue breaths are not given too forcefully or too fast, the air will move through the trachea into the lungs rather than down the esophagus to the stomach. In some cases, air may move into the stomach, however. If the airway is not sufficiently open, if rescue breaths are given too quickly, or if you continue to blow in air even after the lungs have expanded and the chest has risen, then air may be forced into the stomach, making vomiting more likely. Vomiting presents two problems. If an unresponsive victim vomits, you have to roll the victim onto the side to drain the mouth, and then wipe the mouth clean before continuing rescue breathing. Vomiting also increases the risk of aspiration. Although a victim may vomit even with correct rescue breaths, to help prevent vomiting:

- Open the airway before giving a breath.
- Watch the chest rise as you give each breath.
- Blow steadily over 1 second.
- Stop each breath when the chest rises, rather than continuing to blow.
- Let the chest fall between breaths.

Dentures

A victim's dentures are usually left in place during rescue breathing. If they are loose and make it difficult to give breaths or may fall back in the mouth and block the airway, remove dentures before giving rescue breaths.

Facial Injuries

If the victim's mouth cannot be opened or is injured, or if you cannot get a good seal with your mouth over the victim's mouth, you can give rescue breathing through the nose. Hold the victim's mouth closed, seal your mouth over the nose to blow in, and then allow the mouth to open to let the air escape.

Note: A victim with injuries may have blood in the mouth, which needs to be drained before giving rescue breathing. If suction equipment is available and you are trained in its use, you may suction either blood or vomit from the victim's mouth (see Chapter 9).

Conclusion

Basic life support skills used in respiratory emergencies include rescue breathing given by itself or along with chest compressions in CPR. Remember the ABCs and always attend first to an unresponsive victim's airway and breathing. The next chapter describes the BLS skills used in caring for emergencies involving circulation.

Preventing Breathing Emergencies

The common causes of respiratory arrest can often be prevented. They include choking (Chapter 6), drowning, and **sudden infant death syndrome (SIDS)**. In infants and children, most cardiac arrests follow respiratory arrest caused by choking.

Preventing Drowning

About 3,000 people in the United States die each year from drowning. About two-thirds of these are adults and about a third are children under age 14. About three times this number receive emergency treatment for near drowning, and many of these will have permanent disabilities resulting from brain damage caused by lack of oxygen during submersion or related factors.

Drowning is the second leading cause of injury-related death for children 1 to 14 years old. Ninety percent of these drownings occur with an adult "supervising" but typically distracted by other factors. Attentive supervision is the best prevention, including watching infants in bathtubs or near buckets or toilets. Never leave a young child alone in or near a swimming pool, even if the child has had beginning swimming lessons or promises to stay out of the water in your absence. Protective barriers and locked gates are also important.

Half the drowning deaths in adolescents and adults are associated with alcohol use during water recreational activities. Prevention is simple: don't drink and go into or near the water. Swim with a buddy, never dive into shallow or unknown water, and wear a personal flotation device (PFD) in water sports.

About 70% of the annual 750 deaths resulting from boating activities result from drowning. Most victims are not wearing a PFD, and about 40% of cases involve alcohol. Following safe boating guidelines would prevent most of these drowning deaths.

Preventing SIDS

Sudden infant death syndrome (SIDS), the sudden death of an infant under 1 year old of unexplained causes, occurs most commonly between 2 and 4 months of age. SIDS is the most common cause of infant death after 1 month of age. About 2,300 infants die of SIDS in the United States every year. It has been estimated that as many as 900 of the deaths attributed to SIDS each year may have resulted from simple suffocation, because these infants are found in suffocating environments and positions, often lying on the stomach with nose and mouth covered by soft bedding. To reduce the risk of SIDS and suffocation, place infants on their back to sleep. Use a firm, flat crib mattress, and remove pillows, comforters, toys, and other soft objects from the crib. Do not cover the infant's head during sleep. Use only a thin blanket, and tuck it under the edges of the mattress at chest level and below. Avoid smoking—the risk of SIDS is doubled in infants exposed to passive smoke. Maintain a warm temperature in the infant's room, but do not overheat the infant. Give an infant between 1 and 12 months of age a pacifier at bedtime.

Case Scenarios

A. You are called to a scene where a woman is having difficulty breathing. She is gasping and unable to complete a sentence without pausing to breathe. She is sitting and leaning forward, hands on knees.

1. Your first actions should include which of the following?
   a. Start rescue breathing immediately.
   b. Start chest compressions for choking.
   c. Ask her if she has a prescribed medication.
   d. Do nothing yet but wait to see if her condition progresses.

B. You are called to the scene where a man has just been pulled from the water by a co-worker, who has positioned the man lying on his back. The victim is unresponsive, and when you open his airway, you can detect no signs of breathing.

1. What do you do *first?*
   a. Check his pulse.
   b. Using your pocket mask, give him two breaths.
   c. Roll him over and pound his back to get the water out.
   d. Start CPR.

You give him two rescue breaths and watch as his chest rises and falls. You know therefore that his airway is open. But he still is not breathing on his own.

2. What is your next step?
   a. Check his pulse.
   b. Start CPR.
   c. Give abdominal thrusts.
   d. Move him into the recovery position.

You find that he does have a pulse. Another employee is calling for additional help on a cell phone. Because the victim is still not breathing, you will continue rescue breathing.

3. What is the proper way to give rescue breaths to this victim?
   a. Give breaths at a rate of 1 every 3 seconds; take about 1 second to give each breath.
   b. Give breaths at a rate of 1 every 3 seconds; take about 2 seconds to give each breath.
   c. Give breaths at a rate of 1 every 5 to 6 seconds; take about 1 second to give each breath.
   d. Give breaths at a rate of 1 every 5 to 6 seconds; take about 2 seconds to give each breath.

Chapter 5

Basic Life Support 2: Cardiac Emergencies and CPR

As you learned in Chapter 4, basic life support is needed for a victim whose breathing or heart has stopped. Rescue breaths are given to oxygenate the blood in someone whose breathing is inadequate or has stopped. If that victim's heart has stopped, as it will soon after breathing stops, chest compressions also are given to circulate blood to vital organs. Rescue breathing combined with chest compressions is called **cardiopulmonary resuscitation (CPR).** CPR is most commonly given to victims in cardiac arrest as a result of heart attack.

CARDIOVASCULAR DISEASE

Cardiovascular disease includes diseases of the heart and blood vessels. Common diseases include **hypertension** (high blood pressure), **atherosclerosis** ("hardening" and blockage of the arteries often caused by high **cholesterol** levels), and **coronary artery disease** (blockage of the coronary arteries to the heart muscle). Cardiovascular diseases raise the risk of cardiovascular emergencies such as stroke and heart attack, which are two of the top three causes of death, along with cancer. Much cardiovascular disease can be prevented.

CARDIOVASCULAR EMERGENCIES

The two most common cardiovascular emergencies are stroke and heart attack.

Stroke

A **stroke,** also called a cerebrovascular accident (CVA) or a brain attack, is an interruption of blood flow to a part of the brain, killing nerve cells and affecting the victim's functioning. Stroke is a cardiovascular disease that, like heart attack, may be caused by atherosclerosis. About 700,000 Americans a year have a stroke, resulting in over 162,000 deaths and in disability in many stroke victims who survive. Strokes are more common in older adults.

A stroke victim needs medical help immediately to decrease the chance of permanent damage. Therefore it is very important to be able to identify stroke in a victim.

Signs and Symptoms of Stroke

Stroke generally causes a sudden weakness or numbness in the face, arm, or leg on one side; dizziness, confusion, and difficulty understanding speech; and difficulty speaking or swallowing, possibly with vision problems. The victim may experience a sudden, severe headache and may have changing levels of responsiveness or unresponsiveness. The exact signs and symptoms occurring in a stroke victim depend on the site in the brain where an artery is blocked and therefore vary somewhat. The victim's signs and symptoms may mistakenly be attributed to some other condition that affects responsiveness. A screening assessment, such as the Cincinnati Prehospital Stroke Scale, should be used to accurately identify a stroke.

Care for Stroke

The most important thing to do for a stroke victim is to access advanced medical care. Call for help within a healthcare facility, or in an out-of-hospital setting call 9-1-1 immediately. Drugs can often minimize the effects of a stroke—but only if administered very soon. Tell the dispatcher you believe the victim has had a stroke and describe his or her signs and symptoms. Be calming and reassuring to the victim, who often does not understand what has happened and is confused or fearful. Have the victim lie down on his or her back with head and shoulders slightly raised; this is often called the "stroke position" **(Figure 5-1)**. Loosen a constrictive collar. If necessary,

Preventing Cardiovascular Disease

A **risk factor** is anything that makes it more likely that a person will develop a particular disease. Following are known risk factors for cardiovascular disease:

Risk factors that cannot be changed

- Increasing age
- Race
- Hereditary factors

Preventable risk factors

- Smoking
- High cholesterol levels
- High blood pressure
- Physical inactivity
- Obesity and overweight
- Stress

Even though some risk factors cannot be changed, it is important to understand how they increase your risk of cardiovascular disease. In general, the risks of these diseases rise with increasing age. Men are more likely to have cardiovascular disease—although the rates are also high with women, who should not feel immune to heart attacks or other cardiovascular problems. African Americans generally have a higher prevalence of high blood pressure than Caucasian Americans and therefore have a greater risk for cardiovascular disease. Hereditary factors such as a family history of heart disease also can increase one's risk.

If you know that your risk for cardiovascular disease is high because of risk factors beyond your control, this makes it all the more important to prevent those risk factors you *can* control. Risk factors often have an additive effect: the more risk factors you have, the higher your danger overall for developing disease.

Prevention of cardiovascular disease involves eliminating or minimizing risk factors by adopting a healthy lifestyle. In general, this means:

- Not using tobacco
- Eating healthy foods to prevent overweight, help lower cholesterol levels and blood pressure, and help prevent diabetes
- Maintaining low cholesterol levels, with medication when appropriate
- Controlling high blood pressure with diet, exercise, weight control, and medication if needed
- Getting sufficient regular exercise to help prevent overweight, high blood pressure, diabetes, and stress
- Preventing or managing stress

Notice how these risk factors are interrelated. For example, inactivity puts one at risk for being overweight, and weight control also helps prevent hypertension and manage stress. Eating well also helps prevent overweight and control blood pressure. Interrelated risk factors are sometimes referred to as "a constellation" of factors. Similarly, maintaining good cardiovascular health should focus on not only one or two individual factors but a whole constellation of healthy choices that together result in a healthy lifestyle.

turn the victim's head to the side to allow drool or vomit to drain. Monitor the victim and be prepared for vomiting and to give BLS if needed. Move an unresponsive victim into the recovery position and ensure that the airway remains open.

Transient Ischemic Attack (TIA)

A **transient ischemic attack (TIA)**, sometimes called a mini-stroke, is a temporary interruption to blood flow in an artery in the brain. A TIA produces signs and symptoms similar to those of a stroke, except

The Cincinnati Prehospital Stroke Scale

The more quickly stroke is recognized, the more quickly the victim can be given appropriate prehospital care and rushed to a stroke center or other appropriate treatment center. The **Cincinnati Prehospital Stroke Scale (CPSS)** is widely used to identify stroke. The CPSS uses three simple assessments:

1. Ask the victim to smile.

2. Ask the victim to raise both arms out in front of the body.

3. Ask the victim to repeat this sentence: "You can't teach an old dog new tricks."

A victim experiencing a stroke typically manifests these signs:

1. Only one side of the face makes a smile; the other side seems to "droop."

2. One arm drifts away from the position in front of the body.

3. The victim slurs words, uses the wrong words, or cannot speak at all.

In an out-of-hospital setting, also try to learn when the signs and symptoms first occurred. Ask family members or others present at the scene as well as the victim. This information is important for the EMS treatment of the victim.

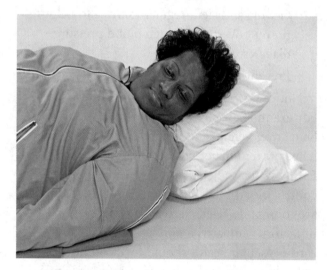

Figure 5-1 Stroke position.

they usually disappear within a few minutes. Since a person who experiences a TIA is at a high risk for a stroke, advanced care should always be given to a victim who exhibits the signs and symptoms of stroke, even if they seem milder or soon disappear.

Heart Attack

Heart attack, or **acute myocardial infarction,** results from a sudden reduced blood flow in the coronary arteries that supply the heart muscle, usually as a result of atherosclerosis. Heart muscle tissue dies in a heart attack. It is a medical emergency and can lead to cardiac arrest. Heart attack can occur at any age.

Signs and Symptoms of Heart Attack

The signs and symptoms of heart attack vary considerably, from vague chest discomfort (which the victim may confuse with heartburn) to crushing pain, with or without other symptoms. The victim may have no signs and symptoms at all before collapsing suddenly. Sometimes the victim has milder symptoms that come and go for two or three days before the heart attack occurs. It is important to consider the possibility of heart attack with a wide range of symptoms rather than expecting a clearly defined situation, including a lack of chest pain or discomfort **(Figure 5-2)**. Note that some heart attack symptoms are more common in women. Chest pain or discomfort is still the most common symptom, but women are somewhat more likely to have shortness of breath, jaw or back pain, and nausea and vomiting. Common signs and symptoms include:

- Complaints of persistent pressure, tightness, ache, or pain in the chest

- Pain may spread to neck, shoulders, or arms

- Shortness of breath

- Dizziness, lightheadedness, feeling of impending doom
- Pale, moist skin or heavy sweating
- Nausea

Care for Heart Attack

It is important to act quickly when the victim may be having a heart attack, because death from heart attack usually occurs within an hour or two after symptoms begin. Care for a victim with heart attack begins with calling for help. In an out-of-hospital setting, call 9-1-1 to get help on the way immediately. Then help the victim rest in the most comfortable position. A sitting position is often easiest for breathing. Loosen any constricting clothing. Try to calm the victim and reassure him or her that help is on the way. Do not let the victim eat or drink anything. Because heart attack frequently leads to cardiac arrest, be prepared to give BLS if needed. Administer supplemental oxygen to the victim if it is available and you are trained in its use (see Chapter 9). Ask the victim if he or she is taking heart medication, and help obtain the medication for the victim.

In recent years the value of aspirin as a clot-preventing medication has become well known,

Facts About Heart Attack

- About 180,000 people a year in the United States die from heart attacks. Many could have been saved by prompt care.
- Heart attack results from coronary artery disease, which can often be prevented or minimized with a healthy diet, exercise, not smoking, control of blood pressure, and regular medical care.
- Heart attack is more likely in those with a family history of heart attacks.
- One-fifth of heart attack victims do not have chest pain—but often have other symptoms.
- Heart attack victims typically deny that they are having a heart attack.

and many healthcare providers advise their patients who are at risk for cardiovascular disease to take one low-dose aspirin daily unless they are allergic or experience side effects such as gastrointestinal bleeding. Some benefit has been demonstrated for aspirin during a heart attack, and for victims who do not need to avoid aspirin, one aspirin is often recommended to be taken when experiencing heart attack symptoms. Rescuers should never on their own give aspirin or any medication to a victim, but may allow the victim to take an aspirin.

Nitroglycerin is often of benefit for a heart attack victim who already has this prescription drug. Nitroglycerin increases blood flow through partially restricted arteries by dilating them. Nitroglycerin is generally prescribed for angina, a condition of pain in the chest caused by narrowed coronary arteries. If the victim has nitroglycerin, you can assist the person in using it. Nitroglycerin comes in small tablets that are dissolved under the tongue, tablets that dissolve in the cheek, extended release capsules, oral sprays, and extended-release patches that are applied to the chest usually daily **(Figure 5-3)**. Follow the victim's instructions to help with the drug. Do not attempt to give the drug yourself if the victim is unresponsive.

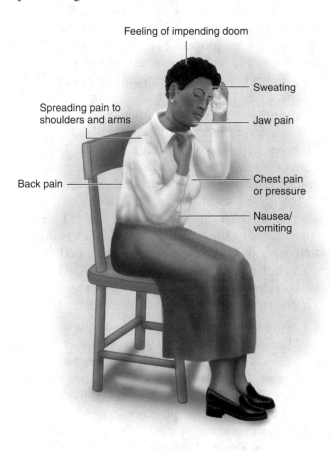

Feeling of impending doom

Sweating

Spreading pain to shoulders and arms

Jaw pain

Back pain

Chest pain or pressure

Nausea/ vomiting

Figure 5-2 Signs and symptoms of heart attack.

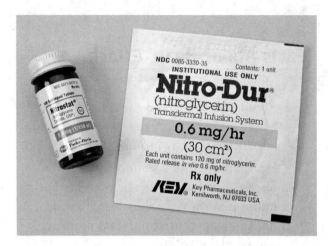

Figure 5-3 Nitroglycerin tablets and patch.

Angina

Angina pectoris, usually just called angina, is chest pain caused by heart disease that usually occurs after intense activity or exertion. Other factors may trigger the pain of angina, such as stress or exposure to extreme heat or cold. The pain is a sign that the heart muscle is not getting as much oxygen as needed, usually because of narrowed or constricted coronary arteries. The pain usually lasts only a few minutes, during which time the person should rest. The pain may also radiate to the jaw, neck, or left arm or shoulder. People usually know when they have angina and may carry medication for it, usually nitroglycerin.

Help a person with angina take his or her own medication and rest. If the pain persists more than 10 minutes or stops and then returns, or if the victim has other heart attack symptoms, give care as for a heart attack.

CARDIAC ARREST

Cardiac arrest may be caused by:

- Heart attack or other heart disease
- Drowning
- Suffocation
- Stroke
- Allergic reaction
- Diabetic emergency
- Prolonged seizures
- Drug overdose
- Electric shock
- Certain injuries

Remember also that respiratory arrest resulting from any cause will soon lead to cardiac arrest.

CPR is used for all victims in cardiac arrest. You do not need to know the cause of cardiac arrest before starting CPR.

CARDIOPULMONARY RESUSCITATION (CPR)

CPR helps keep the victim alive by circulating some oxygenated blood to vital organs. Rescue breaths move oxygen into the lungs, where it is picked up by the blood. Compressions on the **sternum** (breastbone) increase pressure inside the chest, resulting in movement of some blood to the brain and other tissues. The circulation of blood resulting from CPR is not nearly as strong as the circulation from a heartbeat, but it can help keep brain and other tissues alive until a normal heart rhythm is restored. Often an electric shock from an AED (see Chapter 7) or other medical procedures called **advanced cardiac life support** **(ACLS)** are needed to restore a heartbeat—and CPR can keep the victim viable until then. In some instances, the heart may start again spontaneously with CPR.

CPR has clearly been demonstrated to save lives in many circumstances. With the most common cause of cardiac arrest, a heart attack, CPR and defibrillation within 3 to 5 minutes after the victim collapses can save over 50% of victims. Given that sudden cardiac arrest occurs in more than 900 people with heart disease *every day,* CPR followed by AED can clearly be seen to save many thousands of lives every year. Remember that CPR is only one step in the cardiac chain of survival, however: in most cases of cardiac arrest, CPR serves only to keep the victim alive until an AED and/or EMS professionals arrive at the scene.

The general technique of CPR involves alternating chest compressions and rescue breaths. After checking the victim's ABCs and determining that there are no signs of breathing and no pulse, start chest compressions after giving the initial two breaths. For a victim of any age, these are the general steps of CPR (see the Skill: CPR):

1. Find the correct hand position on the lower half of the breastbone midway between the nipples in adults and children **(Figure 5-4)**. In infants, the position is just below a line between the nipples. For adults, place the heel of one hand in the correct position; then put the second hand on top of the first and interlock fingers. For children, depending on their size

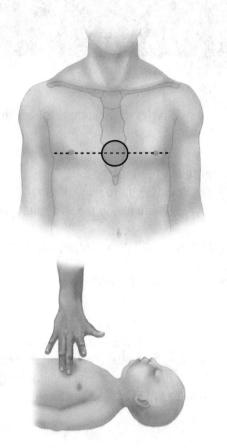

Figure 5-4 Hand placement for chest compressions in CPR.

and your strength, use both hands or the heel of one hand. For infants, use two fingers.

2. Compress the chest hard and fast at a rate of 100 compressions per minute. Compressions in an adult should be 1½ to 2 inches deep. In an infant or child, compressions should be ⅓ to ½ the depth of the chest. Release completely between compressions to let the chest return to its normal height, but do not take your hands or fingers from the chest.

3. If you are alone, alternate 30 chest compressions and 2 rescue breaths for all victims. In two-rescuer CPR for an infant or child, alternate 15 compressions (using the chest-encircling method) and 2 breaths. For all victims, give each breath over 1 second.

Note: If supplemental oxygen equipment is present and you are trained in its use, give the victim oxygen during CPR as described in Chapter 9.

Compressions for Bradycardia in Infant or Child

An infant or child being given rescue breaths or oxygen may have a pulse but still have inadequate

perfusion. If the pulse is under 60 beats per minute and the infant or child has signs of poor systemic perfusion (such as poor skin color), provide CPR with chest compressions. Do not wait for the victim to become pulseless if perfusion is poor even with ventilation with or without supplemental oxygen.

Two-Rescuer CPR for Adults and Children

When two rescuers at the scene are trained in CPR, resuscitation performed by both together offers several advantages. Two-rescuer CPR:

- Minimizes the time between rescue breaths and compressions, making CPR more effective
- Allows for more quickly setting up an AED
- Reduces rescuer fatigue

The first rescuer, who will be giving rescue breaths, begins by checking the victim for responsiveness and breathing. If the victim is not breathing adequately, this rescuer gives 2 rescue breaths as usual, and then checks for a pulse. Meanwhile, the second rescuer ensures that 9-1-1 has been called and moves into position on the opposite side of the victim to give chest compressions.

Two-rescuer CPR is performed in the same cycles of 30 compressions and 2 breaths for an adult (15 compressions and 2 breaths for an infant or child). The first rescuer provides rescue breaths, and the second rescuer gives the chest compressions at a rate of 100 compressions per minute. The second rescuer should count aloud during the compressions and pause after the last compression to let the first rescuer give 2 breaths.

The rescuers should switch positions about every 2 minutes (after 5 cycles of 30 compressions and 2 breaths) to prevent the second rescuer from becoming fatigued and giving ineffective compressions. This change should be done at the end of a full CPR cycle after breaths are given, and should be accomplished in less than 5 seconds.

If an AED is present at the scene, the first rescuer gives both breaths and chest compressions while the second rescuer sets up the unit and attaches the pads (see Chapter 7). If the AED unit advises continuing CPR, the rescuers then give CPR together.

Note: A third rescuer, if present, can give cricoid pressure to help ensure rescue breaths do not go into the stomach and possibly cause vomiting.

Note: You may be assisting a professional with a higher level of training who places an advanced

S k i l l : **CPR**

1 Check the victim's ABCs and determine that the victim is not breathing adequately, has an open airway, and has no pulse.

2 Give 2 rescue breaths, each lasting 1 second. (If the first breath does not go in, reposition the victim's head and try again; if the second breath still does not go in, give choking care (see Chapter 6).

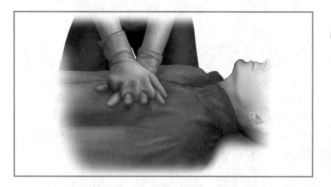

3 Put hand(s) in correct position for chest compressions.

4 Give 30 chest compressions at rate of 100 per minute. Count aloud for a steady fast rate: "One, two, three, . . . " Then give 2 breaths.

5 Continue cycles of 30 compressions and 2 breaths.

6 Continue CPR until:
• The victim begins to move
• An AED is brought to the scene and is ready to use
• Personnel with more training arrive and take over
• You are too exhausted to continue

7 a. If the victim starts moving, check for breathing and a pulse. If the victim is breathing adequately and has a pulse, put the victim in the recovery position and monitor breathing.
b. When an AED arrives, start the AED sequence.

(continued)

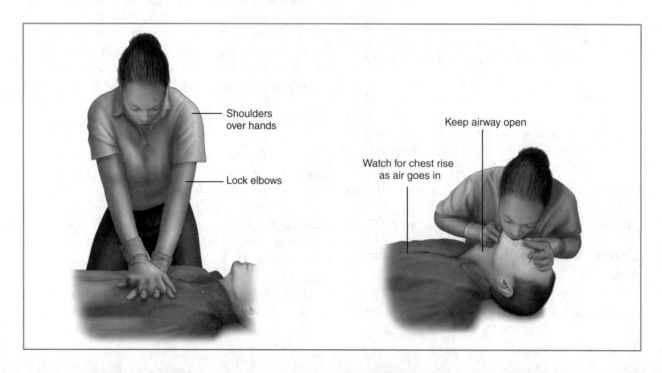

Shoulders over hands

Lock elbows

Keep airway open

Watch for chest rise as air goes in

Skill: **CPR** *(continued)*

Chest Compressions

- Be careful with your hand position for chest compressions. Keep fingers off the chest.
- Do not give compressions over the bottom tip of the breastbone.
- When compressing, keep your elbows straight and keep your hands in contact with the chest at all times.
- Remember to compress the chest hard and fast, but let the chest recoil completely between compressions.
- Minimize the amount of time used giving rescue breaths between sets of compressions.

- Performing chest compressions only is called Hands-Only CPR. It can be used by any bystander to treat adult victims of out-of-hospital, witnessed cardiac arrest. Professional rescuers in a real world role of **bystander** at the scene of an adult victim witnessed cardiac arrest should use the CPR technique that allows them to confidentially deliver good-quality chest compressions with minimal interuption.

---

airway in the victim for ventilation. With an advanced airway in place, chest compressions are given continually, without pauses for rescue breaths. Ventilation (8 to 10 breaths per minute) is provided while compressions are ongoing.

Transitioning from One-Rescuer CPR to Two-Rescuer CPR

In some situations a rescuer is already giving CPR when a second rescuer arrives on the scene. The rescuers should coordinate their actions for a smooth transition from one-rescuer CPR to two-rescuer CPR. The second rescuer moves into position on the other side of the victim to prepare to take over chest compressions. The first rescuer completes a cycle of compressions and breaths. While the first rescuer then pauses to check for a pulse, the second rescuer finds the correct hand position for compressions. When the first rescuer says, "No pulse, continue CPR," the second rescuer begins chest compressions and the first rescuer then gives only rescue breaths. See Skill: CPR for Adult or Child (2 Rescuers).

Note: If you are the first rescuer who started CPR, the arriving second rescuer may be a rescuer with a higher level of training. In such a case this rescuer assumes authority for how CPR should best be continued. If this rescuer determines your

breathing or compression technique is inadequate, he or she may ask you to take on the other role—or may take over the CPR alone.

Two-Rescuer CPR for Infants

Two-rescuer CPR for an infant uses a different hand position for chest compressions. The rescuer giving compressions places the thumbs of both hands together in the correct position on the infant's sternum (just below a line between the nipples). The fingers of both hands encircle the infant's chest (**Figure 5-5**). The chest is compressed with both

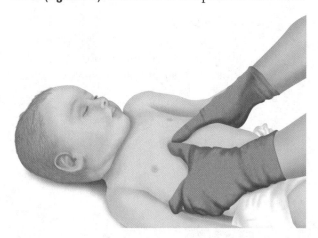

Figure 5-5 The chest-encircling hand position for infant chest compressions when two professional rescuers are giving CPR.

Skill: **CPR for Adult or Child (2 Rescuers)**

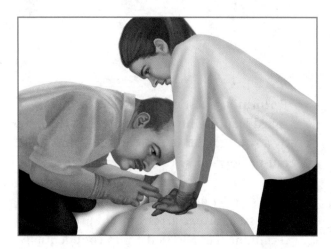

1 At the victim's head, Rescuer 1 checks the victim's ABCs. An AED has been summoned. At the victim's side, Rescuer 2 locates the site for chest compressions.

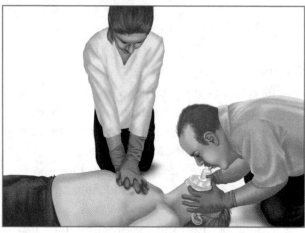

3 Rescuer 1 gives 2 breaths.

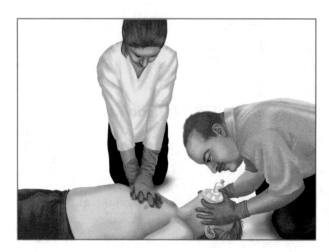

2 Rescuer 1 indicates, "No pulse." Rescuer 2 gives 30 compressions for an adult (15 for a child) at rate of 100 per minute, counting aloud for a fast, steady rate, then pauses.

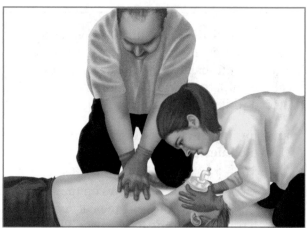

4 Rescuers continue cycles of 30 compressions in an adult (15 in a child) and 2 breaths for about 2 minutes (or after 5 cycles of compressions and ventilations at a ratio of 30:2) before switching compressor and ventilator roles. The switch should be done quickly (in less than 5 seconds).

(continued)

Skill: CPR for Adult or Child (2 Rescuers) *(continued)*

5 Rescuers continue CPR until:
- The victim moves
- An AED is brought to the scene and is ready to use
- Help arrives and takes over

6 If the victim starts breathing and has a pulse, put him or her in the recovery position and monitor the ABCs.

7 If an AED is brought to the scene, start the AED sequence.

Skill: CPR for Infant (2 Rescuers)

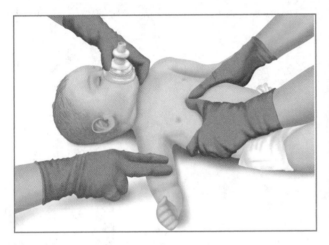

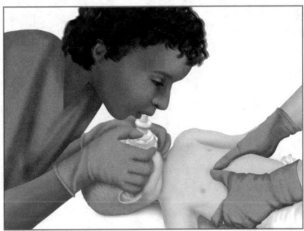

1 At the infant's head, Rescuer 1 checks the ABCs. At the infant's feet, Rescuer 2 locates the site for chest compressions with both thumbs.

2 If pulse is absent, Rescuer 1 says, "No pulse." Rescuer 2 gives 15 chest compressions at a rate of 100 per minute, counting aloud for a fast, steady rate, then pauses.

3 Rescuer 1 gives 2 breaths.

4 Rescuers continue cycles of 15 compressions and 2 breaths for about 2 minutes before switching compressor and ventilator roles. The switch should be done quickly (in less than 5 seconds). Rescuers continue CPR until:
- The infant has a pulse or is breathing
- More advanced help arrives and takes over

5 If the infant starts breathing, hold the infant in the recovery position and monitor the ABCs.

thumbs while the chest is squeezed with the fingers, as described in Skill: CPR for Infant (2 Rescuers).

When Not to Perform CPR

Generally, BLS skills should be performed on any victim who is not breathing and has no pulse. Exceptions in which it is acceptable to not give CPR to a victim include these:

- A Do Not Resuscitate order is present.
- The victim is obviously dead (decapitation, incineration, or clear signs of prolonged death such as rigor mortis).
- It is not safe to be on the scene and the victim cannot be moved somewhere safe.
- A physician pronounces the victim dead.

Conclusion

Remember that, as important as CPR is for sustaining life, in many cases of cardiac arrest the victim also needs defibrillation to restore a normal heartbeat. CPR is also used for unresponsive victims with an airway obstruction, as described in Chapter 6.

Case Scenarios

A. You are called to a scene outside the hospital where an elderly man is sitting on the ground. He is responsive but seems disoriented, and when you ask him how he feels, his words are slurred and he says he has a headache. You decide to screen him for a potential stroke.

1. When you use the Cincinnati Prehospital Stroke Scale, what might you expect to find?
   a. His face looks normal.
   b. When he raises his arms, one arm drifts down.
   c. His blood pressure is falling.
   d. His breath smells fruity.

   The victim does show the signs of having a stroke. You call the emergency department and inform them of the victim's signs and symptoms.

2. What additional care should you provide while waiting for help to arrive?
   a. Have the victim lie down face down with his feet slightly raised.
   b. Have the victim lie down on his back with head and shoulders slightly raised.
   c. Keep him cool and offer water to drink.
   d. Give the victim two aspirin.

B. A co-worker tells you he does not feel very good. He is sweating heavily, although it is not particularly warm, and he seems short of breath. You ask if he feels pain or pressure in his chest, and he says it's not bad, more like indigestion than a sharp pain.

1. Which statement is true?
   a. He may be having a heart attack.
   b. He is not having a heart attack, because he would have crushing chest pain if he were.
   c. He may be having a heart attack, but you should wait 20 minutes before doing anything, to see if his chest symptoms move to his left arm.
   d. He is having a heart attack only if he also experiences nausea.

   You call for additional help, and EMTs have been dispatched.

2. While waiting for their arrival, what else should you do?
   a. Help the victim rest in the most comfortable position.
   b. Keep him up and moving about.
   c. Administer nitroglycerin.
   d. Encourage him to drink water.

(continued)

Case Scenarios (*continued*)

C. As you step out of your vehicle at the scene to which you have been called, you see a group of people standing around a woman on the ground. As you approach, one person tells you he was the first one there; he found the woman motionless on the ground but has no idea what happened. You quickly check her ABCs and find that she is not breathing and has no pulse. You do not carry an AED in your vehicle, but an ambulance has already been dispatched.

1. While positioning the woman on her back, you ask if anyone knows if there is an AED nearby, and one man rushes off to a nearby building to get one. What should you do first?
   a. Give rescue breathing until the AED is brought to the scene.
   b. Call the 9-1-1 dispatcher back and ask for instructions.
   c. Start CPR.
   d. Put her in the recovery position.

2. CPR for this woman should consist of:
   a. Cycles of 15 compressions and 2 breaths, with compressions 1 to $1\frac{1}{2}$ inches deep
   b. Cycles of 15 compressions and 2 breaths, with compressions $1\frac{1}{2}$ to 2 inches deep
   c Cycles of 30 compressions and 2 breaths, with compressions 1 to $1\frac{1}{2}$ inches deep
   d. Cycles of 30 compressions and 2 breaths, with compressions $1\frac{1}{2}$ to 2 inches deep

   You give five cycles of compressions and breaths. She still has no signs of breathing or pulse.

3. What should you do *next?*
   a. Continue with additional cycles of compressions and breaths.
   b. Check her pulse for 30 seconds.
   c. Stop and wait for the AED to arrive.
   d. Speed up the rate at which you are giving compressions.

   A minute or two later another trained professional rescuer arrives at the scene. Neither the ambulance nor the AED has yet arrived. The other rescuer offers to help.

4. How should you transition to two-rescuer CPR?
   a. Stop CPR until the second rescuer is ready, then start anew with one giving rescue breaths and one giving compressions.
   b. Complete the current cycle of compressions, while the second rescuer takes position for compressions when you check for a pulse.
   c. While you are continuing compressions, the second rescuer simultaneously begins to give rescue breaths.
   d. Any of the above is acceptable.

Chapter 6

Basic Life Support 3: Airway Obstruction

An airway obstruction is a life-threatening emergency because the victim is not getting oxygen. Basic life support includes skills to use with a responsive victim who is choking. CPR is used for unresponsive victims with an airway obstruction.

AIRWAY OBSTRUCTION

A victim is said to be choking when the airway is obstructed either partially or fully. A victim can choke on:

- Food or other foreign bodies in the mouth
- The tongue (in an unresponsive victim lying on his or her back)
- Teeth or other body tissues resulting from injury
- Vomit

A complete **airway obstruction** means the victim is getting no air at all and consequently no oxygen into the blood. This victim will soon become unresponsive, and the heart will soon stop. Choking care is urgently needed: the airway must be cleared, and then rescue breathing or CPR must be provided as needed.

With a partial obstruction, the victim is still getting some air into the lungs. The victim may be able to cough out the obstructing object—or breathing may be very difficult, and the victim might be unable to cough strongly enough to expel the object.

ASSESSING CHOKING

Most cases of choking in adults occur while eating. Most cases of choking in infants and children occur while eating or playing. Often, therefore, someone is present and recognizes the choking event while the victim is still responsive.

Choking may be either mild or severe. With a mild obstruction the victim is usually coughing forcefully in an attempt to expel the object. The victim is getting some air and may be making wheezing or high-pitched sounds with breaths, along with coughing. Do not interrupt the person's coughing or attempts to expel the object; do not pound the person on his or her back in an effort to help.

With severe choking, however, the victim is getting very little air or none at all. The person may look frantic and be clutching at his or her throat. You may notice a pale or bluish coloring around mouth and nail beds. A victim who is coughing very weakly and silently, or not coughing at all, is unlikely to expel the obstructing object. The victim cannot speak. Ask the victim if he or she is choking. If the victim cannot answer but indicates that he or she is choking, begin choking care for a responsive victim. This is an urgent situation requiring immediate care.

An unresponsive victim who may be choking is assessed by checking the ABCs as in any unresponsive victim. If the victim is positioned to open the airway but is not breathing, give two rescue breaths. If your first breath does not go into the victim and make the chest rise, try again to open the airway and give a second breath. If it still does not go in, then assume that the victim has an obstructed airway.

CARE FOR CHOKING ADULTS AND CHILDREN

Choking care depends on whether the victim is responsive or unresponsive and whether, in a responsive victim, the obstruction is mild or severe:

- For a **responsive choking victim who is coughing,** encourage the coughing to clear the object. Stay with the victim and call 9-1-1 if the object is not immediately expelled.

- For a **responsive choking victim who cannot speak or cough forcefully,** give abdominal thrusts as described in the Skill: Choking Care for Responsive Adult or Child.
- For **an unresponsive choking victim,** if your rescue breaths do not go in, immediately call (or have someone call) 9-1-1 and begin CPR.

With a responsive victim, after quickly asking for consent and telling the victim what you intend to do, and having someone call 9-1-1, stand behind the victim and reach around his or her abdomen. Having one leg forward between the victim's legs helps you brace in case the victim becomes unresponsive and falls. Keep your head slightly to the side, in case the victim's head snaps back if the victim becomes unresponsive.

Make a fist with one hand, and place the thumb side of the fist against the victim's abdomen, just above the navel. Grasp the fist with your other hand and thrust inward and upward into the victim's abdomen with quick jerks. The pressure of each jerk forces air from the lungs up the trachea to expel the object. Pause only briefly after each abdominal thrust to see if the victim is able to breathe or cough, and continue with additional thrusts if not.

If you are giving abdominal thrusts to a child or someone much shorter than you, kneel behind the victim. If the victim is much taller than you, ask the victim to kneel or sit, because it is important that your thrusts are upward as well as inward, which is impossible if you have to reach up to the victim's abdomen.

Note that because abdominal thrusts can sometimes cause internal injury, it is recommended that a victim who is treated with abdominal thrusts be examined by a healthcare provider.

When a severe obstruction is not cleared, the victim will become unresponsive within minutes. You may have found the victim in an unresponsive condition, or the victim may become unresponsive while you are giving abdominal thrusts if the object is not expelled. In the latter case, quickly and carefully lower the victim to lie on his or her back on the floor. Make sure 9-1-1 has been called. Begin the CPR sequence by opening the airway. When you open the victim's mouth to give a rescue breath, look first for an object in the mouth. If you see an object in the victim's mouth, remove it. If the object is expelled, give two rescue breaths as usual and continue CPR.

If the obstruction remains, the chest compressions of CPR may expel the foreign object. While giving CPR, each time you open the victim's mouth to give breaths, check first to see if an object is visible, and remove it if it is. See the Skill: Choking Care for Responsive Adult or Child and the Skill: Choking Care for Unresponsive Adult or Child.

CARE FOR CHOKING INFANTS

If a responsive choking infant can cry or cough, watch carefully to see if the object comes out. If the infant is responsive but cannot cry or cough, have someone call 9-1-1, and give the infant alternating back slaps and chest thrusts to attempt to expel the object. Support the infant held in one hand against your thigh as you sit or stand, keeping the infant's head lower than the body. To prevent spinal injury, be sure to support the infant's head and neck during these maneuvers. The detailed steps for back slaps and chest thrusts are described in the Skill: Choking Care for Responsive Infant.

If an infant to whom you were giving responsive choking care then becomes unresponsive, send someone to call 9-1-1 and start to give chest compressions. As with an adult or child, the chest compressions may cause the object to be expelled. Check for an object in the mouth before you give a breath, and remove any object you see. Never do a finger sweep of the mouth if you do not see an object, because this could force an object deeper into the throat.

When you encounter an unresponsive infant, first check for breathing as usual. If the infant is not breathing when you have opened the airway, give two breaths. If your first breath does not go in and the infant's chest does not rise, try again after repositioning the infant's head to open the airway. If the second breath does not go in, then assume that the infant has an airway obstruction and provide CPR, checking the mouth for an object each time you open it to give a rescue breath.

Skill: **Choking Care for Responsive Adult or Child**

1   Stand behind an adult victim with one leg forward between the victim's legs. Keep your head slightly to one side. With a small child, kneel behind the child. Reach around the abdomen.

2   Make a fist with one hand, and place the thumb side of the fist against the victim's abdomen just above the navel.

(continued)

Skill: Choking Care for Responsive Adult or Child *(continued)*

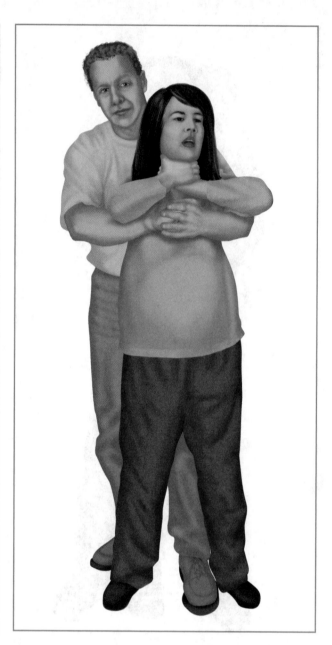

3 Grasp your fist with your other hand and thrust inward and upward into the victim's abdomen with quick jerks. Continue abdominal thrusts until the victim can expel the object or becomes unresponsive. If abdominal thrusts do not succeed in clearing the object from the airway, you may try chest thrusts.

4 For a responsive pregnant victim, or any victim you cannot get your arms around, give chest thrusts in the middle of the breastbone from behind the victim. Take care not to squeeze the ribs with your arms.

Skill: **Choking Care for Unresponsive Adult or Child**

1   Open the airway and determine that the victim is not breathing.

2   Give two rescue breaths, each lasting 1 second. If the first breath does not go in and the chest does not rise, position the victim's head again to open the airway, and try again.

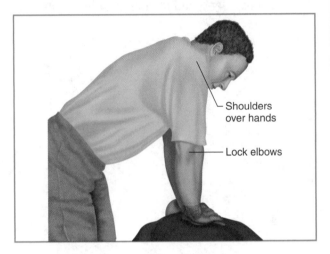

Shoulders over hands

Lock elbows

3   If breaths still do not go in, give chest compressions. Put hand(s) in correct position for chest compressions.

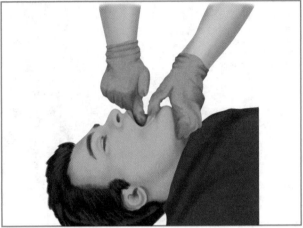

4   Give 30 chest compressions at rate of 100 per minute. Count aloud for a steady fast rate: "One, two, three, . . . " Look inside the mouth before giving breaths after each cycle of compressions, and remove any object you see. Then give two breaths.

5   Continue CPR until:
• The victim begins to move
• Additional help arrives and takes over
• You are too exhausted to continue

Skill: **Choking Care for Responsive Infant**

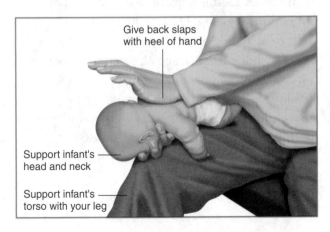

Give back slaps with heel of hand

Support infant's head and neck

Support infant's torso with your leg

1   Support the infant's head in one hand, with the torso on your forearm and your thigh. Give up to 5 back slaps between the shoulder blades.

2   Check for expelled object. If not present, continue with next step.

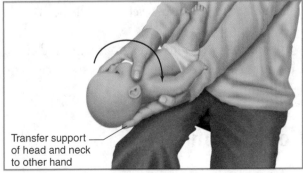

Transfer support of head and neck to other hand

3   With your other hand on the back of the infant's head, roll the infant face up.   *(continued)*

S k i l l : **Choking Care for Responsive Infant (continued)**

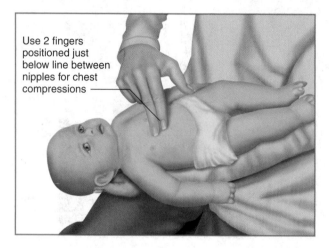

Use 2 fingers positioned just below line between nipples for chest compressions —

5 Repeat steps 1–4, alternating back slaps and chest thrusts and checking the mouth. If alone, call 9-1-1 after 1 minute. Continue until the object is expelled or the infant becomes unresponsive. If the infant becomes unresponsive, give CPR. Look inside the mouth before giving breaths, after each cycle of compressions, and remove any object you see.

4 Give up to 5 chest thrusts with two fingers on sternum. Check mouth for expelled object.

Preventing Choking

Over 4,000 people in the United States die from choking each year. Adults 65 and older are more than twice as likely to die from choking as younger adults, followed by young children.

In adults, choking often results from trying to swallow large pieces of food that have not been chewed sufficiently, eating too quickly, or eating while engaged in other activities. Choking is more common in people under the influence of alcohol or drugs. Choking is also more likely in people wearing dentures, apparently because of a diminished ability to sense how well food has been chewed.

Choking is a serious threat to infants and children up to 3 or 4 years of age, and a significant cause of death. An infant or young child may put any small object in his or her mouth, and nonfood items account for about 70% of choking deaths in infants and young children. Never leave small objects (such as buttons, beads, coins) within reach of an infant. Ensure that small parts cannot break off toys or other items around the infant or young child. Feed infants only soft foods that do not require chewing. Have children sit in a high chair or at a table to eat. Never let a child move around while eating. Teach children not to eat too fast or talk or laugh while eating. Cut into very small pieces any foods a child could choke on, such as hot dogs. Do not give children under age 3 foods such as peanuts, popcorn, grapes, or gum.

Conclusion

So far you have learned the basic life support skills of rescue breaths, CPR, and care for airway obstruction. Chapter 7 describes the final BLS skill: use of an automated external defibrillator (AED) for a victim whose heart is not beating normally.

Case Scenario

You are at lunch in the company cafeteria. An employee has brought her 3-year-old son to work with her today, and they are seated not far from you. Suddenly the woman stands up, yelling for help. As you approach, you see the boy shaking his head frantically, clawing at his neck with both hands. His mother says that he is choking. You identify yourself and ask if you can help.

1. What should you do first?
   a. Confirm that he is not breathing, move behind him, and give abdominal thrusts.
   b. Position him on his back and start rescue breathing.
   c. Have him bend forward against one arm and pound on his back with your other hand.
   d. Give chest compressions the same as in CPR.

While you are providing care, the boy suddenly slumps forward unresponsive. You lower him to the floor on his back.

2. Which of the following actions should you take *first?*
   a. Check his mouth for a foreign body.
   b. Start rescue breathing.
   c. Shout for someone to call for more help.
   d. Give abdominal thrusts.

Another employee has called for more help. You have checked the boy's mouth for a foreign object but see nothing. You position his head to open the airway and try to give a rescue breath, but your breath does not make his chest rise. You reposition his head and try again, and again your air will not go in.

3. What is the next step to take?
   a. Pound on his breastbone with the heel of one hand.
   b. Check his mouth again.
   c. Give CPR starting with chest compressions.
   d. Go to get an AED.

Chapter 7

Basic Life Support 4: AED in Cardiac Emergencies

Not every victim who receives basic life support will benefit from an automated external defibrillator (AED), but many do. In many cases of cardiac arrest, the victim's heart has an abnormal rhythm that does not circulate the blood, and this rhythm can often be corrected with a shock from the AED. Remember the cardiac chain of survival: an AED should be used with any victim who is not breathing and has no pulse.

AEDs and Medical Direction

In many areas a healthcare provider oversees placement and use of the AED, and your AED training must meet certain requirements. For professional rescuers, this is called **medical direction.** Your course instructor will inform you how to meet the current requirements in your area for using an AED.

Laws regarding AEDs are changing. After the FDA approved nonprescription AEDs for home use in 2004, AED units that do not require specific training began appearing in homes and other settings. These devices have been demonstrated for safe use by laypeople who follow the instructions that are printed on the device and are given with sound prompts during use. AEDs have become so simple to use that additional changes in AED regulations may be forthcoming.

The Heart's Electrical System

The heart pumps blood to the lungs to pick up oxygen and pumps oxygenated blood to all parts of the body. The heart has four chambers: the left atrium, the right atrium, and the left and right ventricles. The ventricles, the lower chambers of the heart, do most of the pumping. The heart's electrical system keeps the four chambers of the heart synchronized and working together. The sinoatrial (SA) and atrioventricular (AV) nodes help organize and control the rhythmic electrical impulses that keep the heart beating properly **(Figure 7-1)**. The heart's normal rhythm is called the **sinus rhythm.**

With a heart attack or other heart problems, this rhythmic electrical control may be disrupted, causing an abnormal heart rhythm.

Ventricular Fibrillation

Ventricular fibrillation (V-fib) is the most common abnormal heart rhythm that occurs with cardiac arrest. Although we say a victim in V-fib is in cardiac arrest, the heart is not actually completely still but is beating abnormally. **Fibrillation** means the ventricles of the heart are

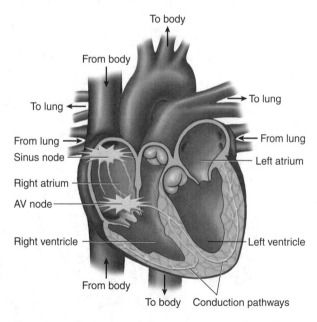

Figure 7-1 The heart.

quivering instead of beating rhythmically. Blood is not filling the ventricles and is not being pumped to the lungs or body as normal.

Since heart attack is the most common cause of cardiac arrest, ventricular fibrillation is a common occurrence. Studies show that in approximately half the cases of cardiac arrest, the victim's heart is in fibrillation and therefore would gain from a shock delivered by the AED.

How AEDs Work

The AED automatically checks the victim's heart rhythm by detecting electrical signals in the body picked up by the AED's **electrodes.** If the victim's heart is in V-fib, the AED will advise giving an electric shock in an attempt to return the heart to a normal rhythm. This is called **defibrillation,** or stopping the fibrillation of the heart **(Figure 7-2)**. The AED's electrodes, or pads, are placed on the victim's chest (or on the front and back of the chest, in a small child), and when the unit delivers a shock, electricity travels to the heart and "jolts" the heart's electrical system, often restoring a normal heartbeat.

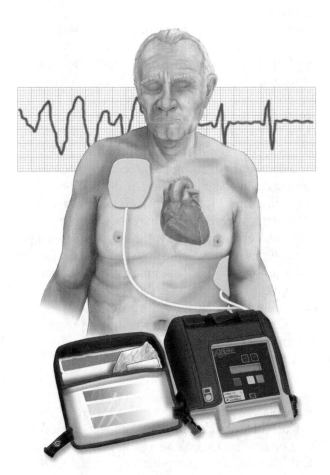

Figure 7-2 An AED gives a shock to the heart.

Contemporary AEDs are easy and simple to use, but they must be used right away. Even when CPR is being given, with every minute that goes by before defibrillation begins, the victim's chances for survival drop by about 10%.

AEDs are complex inside but simple to use. They contain a battery or battery pack and are portable. All units have two pads connected to them with cables. These pads are placed on the victim's chest. The unit then analyzes the victim's heart rhythm and advises whether to give a shock. Some models have a screen that tells you what to do; all models give directions in a clear voice. AED models vary somewhat in other features, but all work in the same basic way **(Figure 7-3)**.

Using an AED

In any situation in which a victim suddenly collapses or is found unresponsive, be thinking about the possibility of cardiac arrest even as you come up to the victim. If someone else is present and you know an AED is available nearby, send that person to get it *now.* It is better to have it right away and not use it than to need it and have to wait for it.

The steps for using an AED are simple:

1. Determine the need for an AED (no response, no breathing, no pulse).

2. Start CPR until the AED is set up and ready to use.

3. Attach the AED to the victim.

4. Analyze the victim's rhythm, and give shock when the unit advises to.

AED and CPR

As always, first check the victim's ABCs. If the victim is not breathing and has no pulse, call for help or send someone to call 9-1-1 and get an AED. Always use an AED if there is no response, no breathing, and no pulse.

Lay rescuers are taught to use the AED on any nonbreathing adult as soon as the unit is available. When two rescuers are present, one should give CPR while the other sets up the AED. Lay rescuers are taught to give 5 cycles of CPR (2 minutes), without a pause to check for a pulse, for a nonbreathing child found unresponsive (not observed to have collapsed suddenly).

For a victim without a pulse, healthcare providers in out-of-hospital settings should also use the AED as soon as it is ready, *except in two situations:*

- For a pulseless child who was not observed to have collapsed suddenly, provide

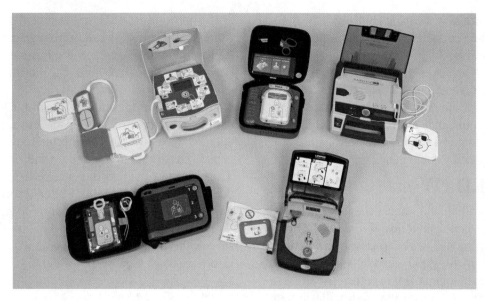

Figure 7-3 A variety of AEDs.

5 uninterrupted cycles of CPR (about 2 minutes) before using the AED.

- For an adult found pulseless on your arrival, when more than 4 to 5 minutes have passed since you were called to respond, provide 5 uninterrupted cycles of CPR (about 2 minutes) before using the AED.

Attach the AED to Victim

Be sure the victim is not in water or in contact with metal. Water or metal conducts electricity that may pose a risk to you or others. Place the AED at the victim's side, next to the rescuer who will operate it. Turn it on, and attach the pads (electrodes) to the victim's chest. Most AED units have a diagram on the pads or the unit itself to remind you where to position them. Typically the first pad is placed on the right side below the collar bone and to the right of the breastbone. The second pad is placed below and to the left of the left nipple and above the lower rib margin.

Attach the AED pads to the victim only if the victim is unresponsive and not breathing and there is no pulse. Expose the victim's chest, and dry the skin if needed with a towel or dry clothing (heart attack victims are often sweating). If the victim has heavy chest hair, quickly shave the pad areas. If a razor is not available, use scissors or trauma shears (which should be kept with the AED) to trim the hair and allow skin contact with the pads. Remove the backing from the pads and apply the pads firmly on the victim's chest.

If required with your AED model, plug the pad cables into the main unit.

Analyze and Shock

With the pads in place and the AED unit on, most AED models then automatically analyze the victim's heart rhythm. Do not move or touch the victim while it is analyzing. After it analyzes the heart rhythm, the unit will advise you whether to give a shock or to continue CPR. If a shock is advised, be sure no one is touching the victim. Look up and down the victim and say, "Everybody clear!" Once everyone is clear, administer the shock (when advised). After the shock, immediately give CPR for 5 cycles (about 2 minutes). Then the AED will analyze again and advise another shock if needed, or continuing CPR (with the pads left in place).

Note that different AEDs may use different prompts. Follow the unit's voice and picture prompts through this process. Some units can be programmed to administer the shock automatically rather than prompt the user to push the shock button; in this case, as always, follow the unit's prompts.

If the victim recovers (moves and is breathing), put an unresponsive, breathing victim in the recovery position and continue to monitor breathing. Keep the AED pads in place, as some victims may return to V-fib and require defibrillation again.

The AED may also say no shock is indicated. This means the victim's heart will not benefit from defibrillation. If so, immediately continue CPR (see the Skill: Using an AED).

Skill: **Using an AED**

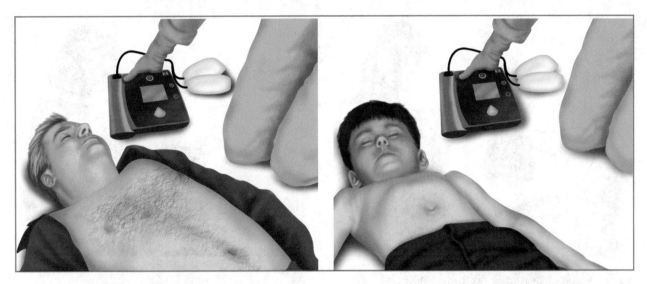

1   Position the victim away from water and metal. Place the unit by the victim's shoulder and turn it on.

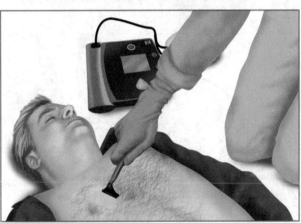

2   Expose the victim's chest, and dry or shave the area if necessary.

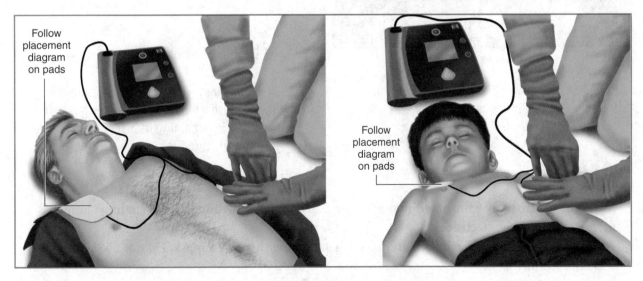

Follow placement diagram on pads

Follow placement diagram on pads

3   Apply pads to the victim's chest. If needed, plug the cables into the unit.

(continued)

S k i l l : **Using an AED** *(continued)*

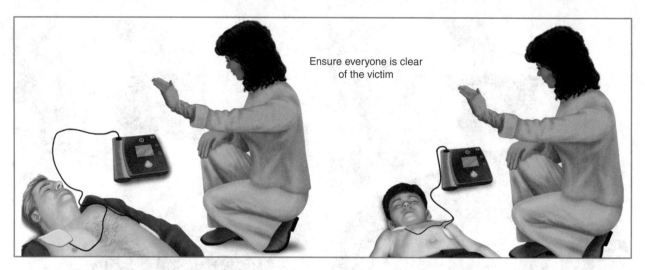

Ensure everyone is clear
of the victim

4 Stand clear during rhythm analysis.

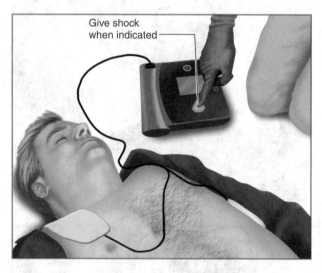

Give shock
when indicated

5 Follow prompts from AED unit to (a) press the shock button or (b) do not shock. Immediately give CPR with the pads remaining in place, starting with chest compressions.

6 Stand clear when the AED prompts to analyze the rhythm again after 5 cycles of CPR (about 2 minutes).

7 Continue steps 5 and 6 until the victim moves or help arrives and takes over.

8 If the victim recovers, put a breathing, unresponsive victim in the recovery position (with pads remaining in place) and continue to monitor the ABCs.

- Move the victim away from standing water before using the AED, and dry the victim's chest well before attaching the electrodes.
- Avoid any flammable materials, including oxygen flowing through a mask. Do not use alcohol to wipe the victim's skin.
- Do not use the AED when in motion in a vehicle or boat.
- Do not use a cell phone or two-way radio within 6 feet of an AED.
- Remember not to touch the victim while the AED is analyzing the rhythm or administering a shock.

AEDs for Children and Infants

Follow the adult guidelines for children over age 8. Although sudden cardiac arrest in younger children is much more rare, it can occur from causes such as:

- Sudden infant death syndrome
- Poisoning
- Drowning
- A heart problem

In most cases, cardiac arrest in a child is not caused by a heart problem, and in most cases the child's heart is not in V-fib. Therefore, give a child 2 minutes of CPR *before* using the AED, unless the child was witnessed to collapse suddenly. If the child does not recover, then use the AED as usual. This is different from the protocol for adults, in whom cardiac arrest is more likely to be the result of heart attack.

In recent years the value of defibrillating a young child in sudden cardiac arrest has been recognized, and pediatric AED electrode pads are now available. It is important to use only approved pediatric AED electrode pads, which are smaller than those for adults and produce lower-energy shocks on a child under age 8. Usually the pads have a distinctive appearance to prevent confusing adult and pediatric pads, such as pink connectors and teddybear emblems. If pediatric pads are not available, however, using adult pads is better than not using the AED at all. Pediatric pads should not be used for an adult, however, because the lower energy is insufficient to affect the heart rhythm.

Be sure to follow the device's instructions for pad placement on a small child. For example, the AED shown on the right in **Figure 7-4** uses pad placement on the front and back of the child's chest. Testing has demonstrated that with small children it can be difficult to position both the pads on the front of the chest, and studies have shown placement on the front and back also delivers an effective shock **(Box 7-1)**.

Currently AED use is recommended both for adults and for children from age 1 to 8. AED use for infants is not recommended against, but the evidence is considered "indeterminate" regarding the benefit of AED use for infants versus the risks of incorrectly analyzing rhythm or delivering an inappropriate shock level. There are proponents of infant AED use, however, and the manufacturers claim AEDs are safe

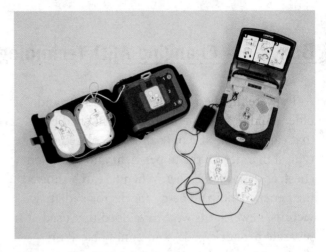

Figure 7-4 Pediatric AED units.

and appropriate for infants when the correct pediatric pads are used.

Special AED Considerations

Situations involving special considerations for the use of an AED include traumatic injuries, hypothermic victims, and the presence of an internal pacemaker or defibrillator or a medication patch. Trauma situations and hypothermia are discussed in Chapter 8.

Internal Pacemaker or Defibrillator

When you expose the victim's chest to apply the AED pads, you may see a bulge or lump beneath the victim's skin from an implanted **pacemaker** or defibrillator, often on the upper left side of the chest **(Figure 7-5)**. Do not place a pad directly over this area, but instead place it at least 1 or more inches away. If the victim's chest or body is jerking, there may be an implanted defibrillator that is giving shocks; wait until jerking has ended before applying the pads.

Medication Patches

If the victim has a medication patch or paste on the chest, remove it and wipe the chest before applying the AED pads **(Figure 7-6)**.

AED Problems and Maintenance

With regular maintenance, an AED should not have any problems during use. The AED may also prompt you to avoid problems. If you get a low-battery prompt, change the battery or battery pack before continuing. Another prompt may

Box 7-1   Changing AED Technology

AEDs were first designed for use on adults and older children and therefore originally had pads that came in one size only and were placed in the typical manner on the upper right and lower left chest, as described earlier. When research showed the benefit of lower-energy shocks for pediatric victims, newer units were developed that used separate pediatric pads, sometimes placed on the front and back of the chest because of the difficulty of pacing both pads far enough apart on the small child's chest. At this time, AED technology continues to evolve, with some new units now able to determine characteristics of the victim and adjust the shock level automatically.

Other new units now use the same pads for all victims, regardless of size and weight, but have a separate switch on the unit to use for pediatric victims. With such advances, separate pediatric pads may eventually become obsolete.

Up through 2005, most AED units used a protocol that advised a series of up to three "stacked" shocks. With technical improvements in AEDs, however, studies showed that a single shock immediately followed by CPR was more effective, and this became the recommended protocol. It is anticipated that AEDs will be reprogrammed to follow this revised protocol, although older units may remain in some settings for a time.

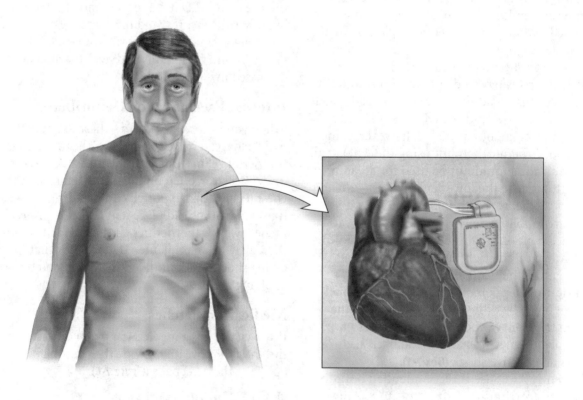

Figure 7-5 Vary AED pad placement if there is an internal device.

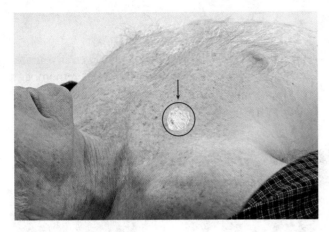

Figure 7-6 Remove medication patches prior to AED pad placement.

advise you to prevent the victim from moving, if the AED detects motion. An error message may also be given if the electrodes are not firmly in contact with the victim's skin.

AEDs require regular maintenance. Check the manual from the manufacturer for periodic scheduled maintenance and testing of the unit. The battery or battery pack must be kept charged, and a charged backup battery or battery pack should be available. Pads should be sealed and replaced on their expiration dates.

A daily inspection of the unit helps ensure the AED is always ready for use and all needed supplies are present. Professional rescuers usually inspect the unit at the beginning of their shift. Most facilities with an AED use a daily checklist form **(Figure 7-7)**. The checklist should always be adapted for the specific AED model, including the manufacturer's daily and periodic maintenance guidelines. In addition, many units come with a self-diagnostic test or simulator device to be used to check that the AED is correctly analyzing rhythms and delivering shocks; this may be part of the daily inspection routine.

AED INSPECTION CHECKLIST

Date: _____ Location: _____ AED Model: _____

Inspected by: _____ Signed: _____

Criteria	ok/no	Corrective action/remarks
AED unit		
verify correctly placed	____	_____
clean, clear of objects	____	_____
no cracks or damage to case	____	_____
cables/connectors present and not expired	____	_____
fully charged battery in place	____	_____
charged spare battery present	____	_____
check status/service light indicator	____	_____
check absence of service alarm	____	_____
power on, self-test	____	_____
Supplies		
Two sealed sets of electrode pads	____	_____
Verify expiration date on pad packages	____	_____
Razor	____	_____
Medical exam gloves	____	_____
Hand towels	____	_____
Alcohol wipes	____	_____
Scissors	____	_____
Pocket mask or face shield	____	_____

Figure 7-7 Example of an AED inspection checklist.

Conclusion

You have learned how rescue breathing, CPR, and AED work together in the treatment of victims in cardiac arrest **(Table 7-1)**. These are crucial skills for professional rescuers, and they also require periodic refreshing in order to remain effective. Even if you are now becoming certified in CPR and AED, remember that to continue to use these lifesaving skills in the future, you will eventually need a refresher course.

Table 7-1

Summary of Basic Life Support

Step	Infant (under 1 year)	Child (1–puberty except 1–8 for AED)	Adult
1. Check for responsiveness.	Stimulate to check response.	"Are you okay?"—Tap shoulder.	
2. If unresponsive, call for help.	Send someone to call 9-1-1. Give 2 minutes of care before calling 9-1-1 yourself if alone.	Send someone to call 9-1-1. Give 2 minutes of care before calling 9-1-1 yourself if alone (except for known heart problem).	Send someone to call 9-1-1. Call 9-1-1 immediately if alone (give 2 minutes of care first for victim of drowning, poisoning, injury).
3. If unresponsive: Open airway.	Head tilt–chin lift (but do not overextend neck).	Head tilt–chin lift or jaw thrust.	
4. Check breathing.	Look, listen, feel for breathing.		
5. If not breathing: Give 2 breaths, watch chest rise.	Use barrier device or cover mouth, nose, or stoma. Each breath lasts 1 second.		
6. If chest does not rise with first breath: Reposition airway and try again.	Each breath lasts 1 second.		
7. If chest still does not rise: Start care for airway obstruction.	Start CPR, beginning with chest compressions. Check mouth for object each time breaths are given.		
8. If chest rises with breaths: Check for a pulse.	Check for brachial or femoral pulse.	Check for carotid pulse.	
9. If a pulse is present but no breathing, give rescue breathing.	1 breath every 3–5 seconds.		1 breath every 5–6 seconds.
10. If no pulse, give CPR.	For compressions, use 2 fingers just below line between nipples. Compress chest $\frac{1}{3}$ to $\frac{1}{2}$ the depth of chest.	For compressions use one or two hands midway between nipples. Compress chest $\frac{1}{3}$ to $\frac{1}{2}$ the depth of chest.	For compressions use both hands, one on top of other, midway between nipples. Compress chest $1\frac{1}{2}$–2 inches.
Chest compressions:	Rate of 100 per minute. Cycles of 30 compressions and 2 breaths (except 15:2 in two-rescuer CPR for infant or child).		
11. Infrequently check for breathing and pulse.	Look, listen, and feel for breathing. Check pulse.		
12. Use AED when available (if no breathing and no pulse).	Not recommended.	Use pediatric electrode pads.	Use adult AED electrode pads.
13. If victim recovers adequate breathing and pulse, put in recovery position.	Hold infant and monitor ABCs.	Lay on side in recovery position and monitor ABCs.	

Case Scenario

You and your partner respond to a home where a man in his 40s has collapsed. Your partner is carrying the AED as you enter the house. The victim is on his side on the floor. His wife tells you he suddenly just passed out and fell to the floor—about 6 minutes ago. You position the unresponsive victim on his back.

1. What do you do *first?*
   a. Open his airway and check for breathing.
   b. Check for a pulse.
   c. Start CPR.
   d. Help your partner set up the AED.

You discover he is not breathing. Your first two breaths go in. You check for, but do not find, a pulse. Your partner has the AED almost ready to use.

2. Now what should you do?
   a. Dry his chest so he is ready for the AED pads.
   b. Give rescue breathing.
   c. Provide 5 cycles of CPR (about 2 minutes).
   d. Put him in the recovery position.

After the 2 minutes of CPR, your partner has applied the AED pads to the victim's chest. She tells you the unit is ready to analyze the victim's heart rhythm.

3. What should you now be doing at this moment?
   a. Continue CPR until the unit completes its analysis.
   b. Ask your partner to assist you with CPR while the unit does the analysis.
   c. Give another 2 minutes of CPR before having the unit analyze his rhythm.
   d. Do not touch the victim during the analysis.

The AED advises giving a shock. You stay clear of the victim, and your partner presses the button to administer a shock.

4. What is now your appropriate action?
   a. Take up to 30 seconds to check for a pulse.
   b. Continue CPR.
   c. Administer another shock.
   d. Put the victim in the recovery position.

(continued)

Case Scenario (*continued*)

After 2 minutes of CPR, the AED analyzes the victim's rhythm again and does not advise a shock. You continue two-rescuer CPR with the pads still in place, and after about 2 more minutes the victim's chest moves. You check his ABCs and find he is now breathing adequately and has a pulse. He remains unresponsive.

5. What do you do now?
   a. Remove the AED pads and keep the victim on his back with his head tilted to keep his airway open.

   b. Tell your partner to pack up the AED and return it to your vehicle while waiting for help to arrive.

   c. Put the victim in the recovery position with the pads still in place, and monitor his breathing and pulse.

   d. Continue CPR.

Chapter 8

Special Resuscitation Situations

In most emergencies, basic life support skills are used in the same way. Check the victim's ABCs and provide care as needed, including opening the airway, checking breathing and giving rescue breaths if needed, and providing CPR and using an AED for cardiac arrest. A few situations, however, involve special considerations in the use of these skills or the approach to the victim.

TRAUMA

In most situations in which the victim is severely injured by blunt or penetrating trauma, problems with the airway, breathing, or circulation are the result of the trauma rather than a coinciding problem. Do not assume, however, that a trauma victim has experienced *only* trauma, because another problem may have occurred first or at the same time. For example, a victim may have a heart attack and sudden cardiac arrest while on a ladder, resulting in a fall and possible fractures. A victim of drug overdose or poisoning may develop a severe breathing problem while operating machinery, causing an accident and traumatic injury. As a general rule, treat a trauma victim like any other: check the ABCs and give basic life support as needed.

Trauma victims generally have a *call first* rather than *call fast* status. Trauma that is severe enough to cause cardiac arrest usually requires surgical correction, so the victim needs to be transported to definitive care as quickly as possible.

Depending on the nature of the trauma, the victim may have a spinal injury as well. Any blow to the body severe enough to impact the airway, breathing, or circulation is likely also to potentially injure the spine. Remember to keep the head in line with the body when positioning the victim, and use the jaw thrust technique rather than head tilt–chin lift to open the airway.

Trauma to the head or face may result in blood or other fluid blocking the airway. Check the mouth when opening the airway, and if necessary wipe out any blood or vomit. With more extensive fluid, you may have to turn the victim onto one side to let it drain from the mouth. If the equipment is available and you are trained in its use, suction the victim's mouth when opening the airway (see Chapter 9).

In cases of cardiac arrest in victims with severe trauma, local protocol may include not using the AED, since these victims seldom have a heart rhythm that can be corrected. Always follow your local protocol, and if the AED is not used, give CPR as usual while waiting for advanced help.

HYPOTHERMIA

Hypothermia is a low body core temperature as a result of exposure to a cold environment, often by immersion in cold water. Hypothermia requires special consideration as it may cause breathing and pulse to be difficult to find. It may make the victim susceptible to heart rhythm problems, because victims have been successfully resuscitated after a long period of hypothermia or immersion.

In severe hypothermia, the victim's heart may be beating very slowly or may be in arrest, and the respiratory rate too may be very slow or have stopped. The victim may appear to be dead. Take extra time as needed to check for breathing and up to 30 to 45 seconds to find a pulse. If the victim has no pulse, start CPR as usual. Follow local protocol for use of an AED with a hypothermia victim. Typically only one shock is given while the victim is cold; CPR and rewarming continue, and the AED may be used again when the core temperature has risen to 86 to 90° F (30° to 32° C).

Do not delay or stop resuscitation efforts to rewarm the victim, but if possible prevent further heat loss from the victim's body. Other rescuers can remove wet clothing, for example, or cover the victim with a blanket while basic life support is ongoing. Be gentle when handling or moving a hypothermic victim, because the heart is susceptible to dysrhythmias precipitated by motion or jarring.

Near Drowning

In any situation in which a victim is in the water, ensure your own safety before attempting a rescue. It is very dangerous for an untrained rescuer to enter the water to rescue a responsive victim, who may grab the rescuer and make rescue difficult or impossible. Reach to the victim with a pole or long object, throw a rope or floating object, or go to the victim in a watercraft if possible. Beginning rescue breaths as soon as possible is a high priority for drowning victims. If you can do so, begin rescue breaths (after confirming respiratory arrest) even before removing the victim from shallow water. It is necessary to remove the victim from water, however, to give CPR.

With an unresponsive victim removed from the water, consider whether the nature of the incident suggests a possible spinal injury, such as diving in shallow or murky water or being thrown against the shore in surf conditions. If the cause of the submersion is unknown, assume the victim may have a spinal injury. Keep the head in line with the body when moving or positioning the victim, and use the jaw thrust technique rather than a head tilt–chin lift to open the airway.

Check the ABCs as usual. Remember that this is a *call fast* rather than *call first* situation. If you are alone, give 5 cycles of CPR (about 2 minutes) before stopping to go for help.

The victim may need rescue breathing or CPR. Give basic life support as usual—do not try to remove water from the victim first. If the victim is not breathing and your rescue breaths do not make the chest rise, a foreign body may be obstructing the airway. Check inside the mouth and remove any foreign body. Open the airway again and try to give 2 breaths. If your breaths still do not go in, give chest compressions for an airway obstruction. Do not try to take other actions to remove suspected water from the lungs.

If supplemental oxygen is available and you are trained in its use, administer oxygen to the victim (see Chapter 9). When an AED is available and is ready to use, use it as usual. Victims have been resuscitated after being submerged in cold water for some time. If the victim may be hypothermic, follow the special considerations described earlier.

Electric Shock

Electric shock may result from a lightning strike or contact with a source of household current or high-voltage power lines. The shock may cause breathing to stop because of paralyzed respiratory muscles and may cause cardiac arrest by disrupting the heart's electrical controls.

Remember scene safety before approaching the victim. Downed power lines or household or industrial electrical appliances or cords may still be "live" and pose a threat to rescuers. Call 9-1-1 for downed power lines, and do not attempt to move them yourself or move the victim away from them. With electrical appliances, first shut the power off at the circuit breaker box or unplug the power cord if it is safe to do so.

The electrical shock may cause a range of injuries in addition to effects on respiration and circulation. Especially with a high-voltage shock, such as that caused by lightning, the victim my have severe burns and possible fractures due to strong muscular contractions caused by the electrical shock. With a lightning strike victim, assume that there may be spinal injury.

When it is safe to approach the victim, check his or her ABCs and provide care as needed. If the victim has a pulse but is not breathing, provide rescue breathing and continue to check the pulse. If the victim has no pulse, provide CPR and call for an AED. Often an electrical shock causes ventricular fibrillation, in which case the AED may return the heart to a normal rhythm. If alone, shout for help and for an AED to be brought, but give 5 cycles of CPR (about 2 minutes) before stopping to go for help.

Pregnancy

As described in Chapter 6, a woman in late stages of pregnancy with an airway obstruction should be given chest thrusts rather than abdominal thrusts to expel an obstructing object. A responsive victim can be given chest thrusts from behind while standing, and an unresponsive victim is given chest thrusts in the same manner as the chest compressions of CPR. Note that chest compressions should be given slightly higher on the sternum in a pregnant woman.

When a pregnant woman at a gestational age beyond 20 weeks lies on her back, the enlarged uterus may press against the inferior vena cava, which returns blood to the heart from the lower half of the body. This pressure may decrease the blood flow to the heart and affect circulation to vital organs. When possible, therefore, position an injured pregnant woman lying on her left side, which reduces pressure from the uterus on the vena cava. Gently move the uterus to the left to help alleviate the pressure.

When giving CPR to a pregnant woman at a gestational age beyond 20 weeks, if possible position her for chest compressions on a firm surface that can be tilted so that her back is angled back 15 to 30 degrees from the left lateral position (lying on left side).

Otherwise, perform basic life support skills on a pregnant woman in the same manner as other victims, including use of an AED in cases of cardiac arrest.

Conclusion

The special considerations described in this chapter do not contradict the techniques of basic life support as detailed throughout this text. In all situations the professional rescuer should check the scene for safety before approaching the victim, should first check the victim's ABCs, and should give BLS care as needed. In these circumstances, however, rescuers may slightly adapt their care because of special needs or characteristics of the victims.

Case Scenarios

A. You are first on the scene where a 10-year-old boy has just been pulled from the icy cold water after he broke through the ice more than 20 minutes ago. He is unresponsive, and his skin is very cold and pale. You gently position him on his back and open his airway. After 10 seconds you have not detected breathing.

1. What should you do *next*?
   a. Start CPR immediately.
   b. Check for a pulse for up to 30 to 45 seconds.
   c. Wait for the AED to arrive.
   d. Move him indoors to start the process of rewarming.

The victim is determined to be in cardiac arrest. You have given CPR for about 2 minutes when another responder arrives with an AED, blankets, and oxygen equipment.

2. Which aspect of care is now the *highest* priority?
   a. Dry the victim and use the AED.
   b. Hook up oxygen to the resuscitation mask and continue CPR.
   c. Wrap the victim in blankets.
   d. Turn victim face down and pump his back to drain water from lungs.

B. In an equipment room you find a woman on the floor, her hand on an electric appliance's frayed cord on the floor. There is what looks like a burn mark on her hand. She does not respond when you call her name.

1. What do you do *first*?
   a. Tap her on the shoulder and ask, "Are you okay?"
   b. Check her ABCs.
   c. Make sure the power to the appliance is turned off.
   d. Start CPR immediately.

You shut off the power at a nearby circuit breaker, then quickly check her ABCs. She is not breathing and has no pulse. You are alone in the room.

2. What should you do *next*?
   a. Shout for help and give 5 cycles of CPR (about 2 minutes) before stopping to call for additional help if no one comes to the scene.
   b. Telephone immediately for an AED to be brought.
   c. Treat the burn on her hand, and then recheck her ABCs.
   d. Leave her and run for the nearest AED.

Chapter 9

Advanced Resuscitation

In most emergency situations, professional rescuers can provide basic life support without specialized equipment or supplies beyond basic personal protective equipment such as gloves and a resuscitation mask. Several adjunctive devices, however, can enhance the effectiveness of resuscitation. These devices include suction devices to help keep the victim's airway clear, oral and nasal airways to help ensure that air reaches the victim's lungs, bag mask units for more effective rescue breathing, and supplemental oxygen.

The resuscitation adjuncts you may use depend on both your training and your job description. As well, these devices may not be available in the emergency setting where you are caring for a victim. It is essential, therefore, to be able to perform BLS techniques such as rescue breathing and CPR without special equipment, as described in earlier chapters. In addition, resuscitative measures should never be delayed while waiting for adjunctive equipment.

When these devices are available and you are trained in their use, adjunctive devices do increase the efficiency of resuscitation techniques and increase the victim's chances for full recovery.

SUCTION DEVICES

A **suction device** is used to clear blood, vomit, and other substances from a victim's airway. These devices are generally safe and easy to use. Although different types of suction devices are available, they are similar in their use. Manual devices develop suction with a hand-pumping action, while other devices are powered by a battery or pressurized oxygen. Soft rubber bulb syringes are used for suctioning infants.

Suction devices for adults and children have a clear plastic tip that is inserted into the mouth or nostrils to suck out fluids and small solids. Different suction tips are available, varying from small, soft plastic tips that are more effective with fluids to larger, more rigid tips more effective for vomit and particulate matter. Some devices have a suction control port at the base of the tip that you cover with your finger to produce suction. As always, you should be familiar in advance with the specific equipment you may use in an emergency.

Suction is useful whenever a victim's airway may be obstructed—fully or in part—by body fluids, vomitus, or other matter. If the victim vomits when rescue breathing or CPR is under way, or if secretions or blood accumulate and impede ventilation, stop and quickly suction the mouth and/or nose and then continue the resuscitation. An unresponsive breathing victim may also need suctioning to maintain an open airway. Usually you know that the airway needs suctioning when you hear gurgling sounds during breathing or ventilation.

The victim's head is turned to the side to help drain vomit or fluids before suctioning. If the victim may have a spinal injury, the victim must be turned on the side with the head and body in line as a unit, with the help of other rescuers. See Skill: Suctioning (Adult or Child) and Skill: Suctioning (Infant).

S k i l l : **Suctioning (Adult or Child)**

1 Confirm that the suction device is working and produces suction.

2 Turn the victim's head to one side and open the mouth (with spinal injury, support the head and turn with body as one unit).

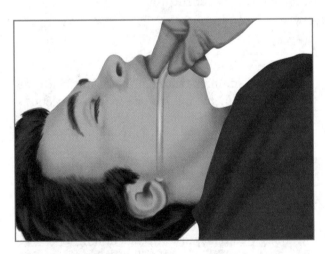

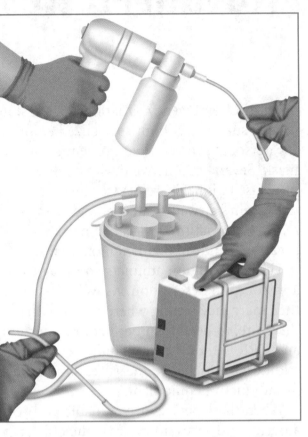

3 Sweep out solids and larger amounts of fluid with your finger.

5 Turn on the suction, or pump the handle to create suction.

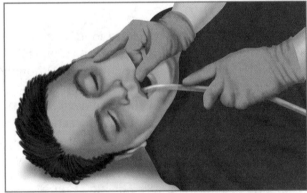

4 Determine the maximum depth of insertion by measuring the catheter tip from the earlobe to the corner of the mouth.

6 Insert the catheter tip carefully into the mouth. Put your finger over the proximal opening to begin suctioning, and move the tip about as you withdraw it.

7 Reposition the victim's head with airway open, and begin or resume rescue breathing or CPR if needed.

Skill: **Suctioning (Infant)**

1   Hold the infant in position for suctioning, with the head lower than the body and turned to one side.

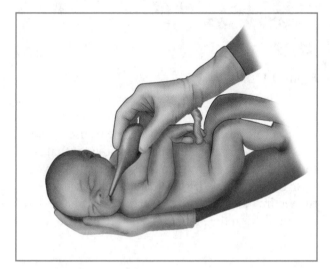

2   Squeeze the suction bulb first and then gently insert the tip into the infant's mouth.

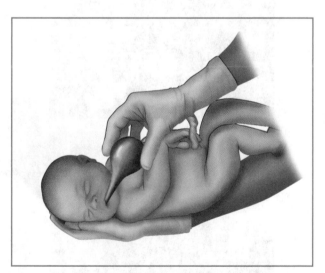

3   Gradually release the bulb to create suction as you withdraw the tip from the infant's mouth.

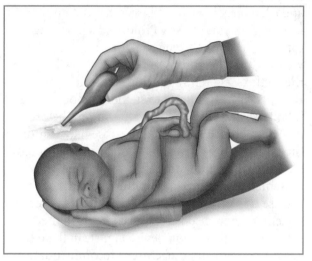

4   Move the bulb aside and squeeze it, with tip down, to empty it.

5   Repeat steps 2 to 4 until the airway seems clear, up to 3 times.

6   Repeat the suctioning steps for each nostril.

7   Begin or resume rescue breathing or CPR if needed.

Safety precautions are necessary when suctioning. Because many suction devices generate strong suction pressures, be careful with the suction tip. Prolonged contact with mucous membranes in the mouth and nose can cause bruising, swelling, and even bleeding. Never insert the suction tip farther than you can see. Prolonged suctioning can also decrease the volume of air reaching the victim's lungs. Vigorous suctioning may stimulate the victim's gag reflex, causing additional vomiting. Be especially careful not to suction too deep in an infant. Always suction an infant's mouth before the nostrils, because suctioning the nose may stimulate the infant to breathe in and thereby inhale fluid or secretions from the mouth.

Remember standard precautions against disease transmission through body fluids. After the emergency, dispose of any contents in the reservoir of the suction device and clean the device according to the manufacturer's recommendations.

AIRWAY ADJUNCTS

Oral and nasal **airways** are devices that help keep a victim's airway open during resuscitation or until the victim receives advanced medical attention. As discussed in Chapter 3, the most common cause of airway obstruction in unresponsive victims is the tongue. An airway device prevents this problem, and keeps the airway open more easily than head position alone while using resuscitation techniques or caring for a breathing victim. Supplemental oxygen can be given through a resuscitation mask or bag mask with an airway in place.

Oral Airways

Oral airways, also called **oropharyngeal airways,** are used only in unresponsive victims who do not have a gag reflex. If inserted into a responsive victim, or one who still has a gag reflex, the airway adjunct can cause vomiting. The victim's airway must be opened before the airway device is inserted; the device does not open the airway itself but will help keep it open. An oral airway can be used in an unresponsive victim who is breathing or who is receiving rescue breaths.

Proper placement of the oral airway is essential. An improperly placed airway device can compress the tongue into the back of the throat and further block the airway. Oral airways are curved so that they fit the natural contour of the mouth and are available in various sizes to ensure a proper fit **(Figure 9-1)**. An airway adjunct that is too big can

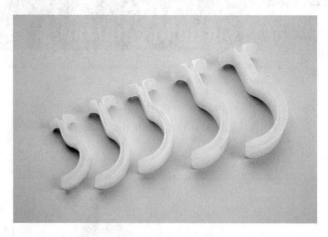

Figure 9-1 Oral airways.

cause vomiting and may prevent the resuscitation mask from sealing well. An airway adjunct that is too small can slide into the back of the pharynx and obstruct the airway **(Figure 9-2)**. Remember to open the victim's airway before inserting the oral airway, as described in the Skill: Oral Airway Insertion.

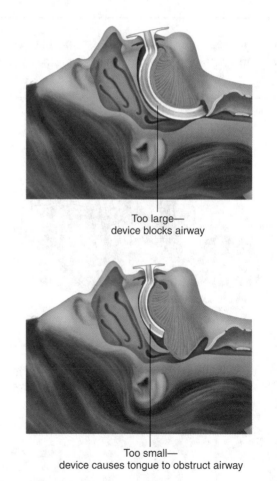

Too large—
device blocks airway

Too small—
device causes tongue to obstruct airway

Figure 9-2 An oral airway that is too large or too small will obstruct the airway.

Skill: **Oral Airway Insertion**

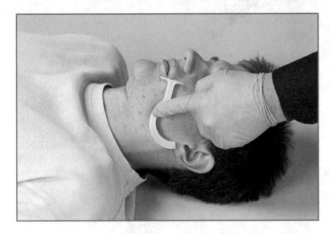

1 Choose an airway device of the correct size.

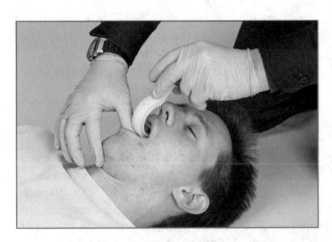

2 Open the victim's airway with a head tilt–chin lift or a jaw thrust, and open the mouth. Insert the airway device with the tip pointing toward the roof of the mouth.

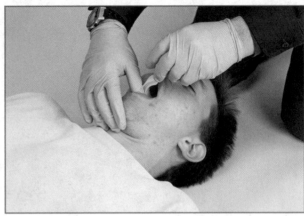

3 When the tip reaches the back of the mouth and you feel resistance, rotate the airway 180 degrees.

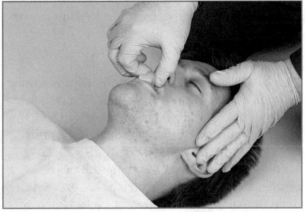

4 Continue to insert the airway device to final position (with the flange resting on the lips).

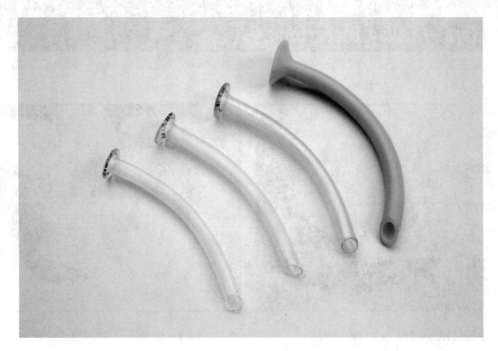

Figure 9-3 Nasal airways.

Periodically reassess the airway adjunct to confirm that it remains in proper position. A victim can be suctioned with an oral airway in place.

Nasal Airways

A nasal airway, like an oral airway, helps maintain an open airway **(Figure 9-3)**. A nasal airway (**nasopharyngeal airway**) can be used in a victim who is responsive or who, although unresponsive, has a gag reflex. Nasal airways are also effective for unresponsive victims with mouth or jaw injuries or tightly clenched teeth that prevent use of an oral airway. Nasal airways are less likely to cause gagging and vomiting than oral airways, but a disadvantage is that they are too narrow to suction through easily. Insert a nasal airway as described in the Skill: Nasal Airway Insertion, and continue to keep the victim's airway open with the head tilt–chin lift or jaw thrust. If needed, suction through a nasal airway using a small flexible suction catheter.

RESUSCITATION MASKS AND BAG MASKS

Whether given by itself or as part of CPR, rescue breathing is performed more safely and effectively with a face mask. By using a mask, the rescuer avoids direct contact with the victim's mouth and thereby minimizes the risk of bloodborne and airborne disease transmission. The mask also makes it easier to ventilate the victim. The two primary types of masks used in emergencies are the resuscitation mask and the bag mask.

The resuscitation mask, often called a pocket face mask or simply a face mask, seals over the victim's mouth and nose and has a port through which the rescuer blows air to give rescue breaths. A one-way valve in the port allows the rescuer's air to enter through the mouthpiece, but the victim's exhaled air exits the mask through a different opening. The rescuer's mouth is thereby protected from infection by the victim's air or body fluids. Chapter 4 describes how to seal a face mask to the victim's face and hold it in place. Face masks also have a port to which oxygen tubing can be connected so that supplemental oxygen can also be delivered through the mask. A face mask can also be used with an oral or nasal airway in place.

Bag mask (BVM) units also protect the rescuer but are more effective for providing ventilations to nonbreathing victims because the victim receives air from the atmosphere (21% oxygen) rather than air the rescuer exhales (16% oxygen). The more oxygen delivered to the lungs, the more oxygen will reach the victim's vital organs to maintain life. Several different types of

S k i l l : **Nasal Airway Insertion**

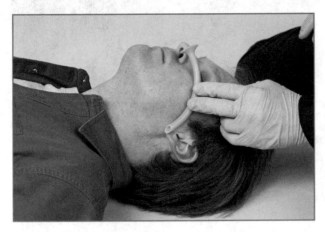

1   Choose the correct nasal airway size.

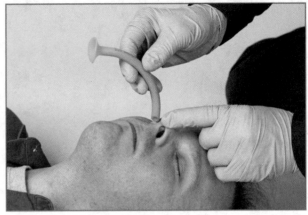

3   Insert the nasal airway in the right nostril with the bevel toward the septum.

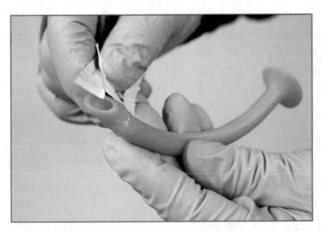

2   Coat the nasal airway with lubricant.

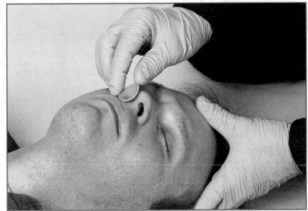

4   Insert the nasal airway straight back, sliding it along the floor of the nostril.

5   Insert the nasal airway until the flange rests against the nose.

Figure 9-4 A typical bag mask (BVM) unit.

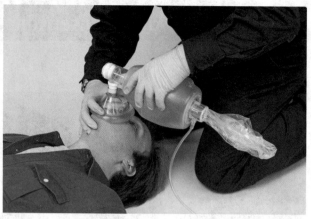

Figure 9-5 A single rescuer can use the BVM to provide rescue breathing, although use by two rescuers is recommended.

BVM units are available, but each has at least three components **(Figure 9-4)**:

- The self-inflating bag holds the air or oxygen that is delivered to the victim when the bag is squeezed.
- The one-way valve allows air or oxygen to flow from the bag to the victim but prevents the victim's exhaled air from returning to the bag.
- The mask is similar to a resuscitation mask and is connected to the bag and valve; the proper size mask must be used for a proper fit.

An oxygen reservoir bag may be attached to the other end of the bag when supplemental oxygen is used.

To use the BVM on a nonbreathing victim, position yourself above the victim's head. Perform a heat tilt, and then position the mask on the victim's face. If you are alone, you need to hold the mask with one hand and squeeze the bag with the other, as shown in **Figure 9-5**. To hold the mask in place with one hand, use the C-clamp technique, with thumb and index finger on the edges of the mask while the other fingers lift the jaw into the mask. When a second rescuer is available to help with the BVM, one rescuer holds the mask in place using both hands. Two-rescuer use of the BVM is recommended whenever possible because of the difficulty one person may have sealing the mask on the victim's face with one hand while squeezing the bag with the other.

With the mask sealed in place, rescue breaths are delivered to the victim by squeezing the bag.

Squeeze a 1-liter adult bag about ½ to ⅔ of its volume. Squeeze a 2-liter adult bag about ⅓ its volume. Squeeze the bag over 1 second, watching the victim's chest rise. Give a ventilation every 5 to 6 seconds in an adult (or every 3 to 5 seconds in an infant or child), the same as with rescue breathing by mouth or resuscitation mask.

When using a BVM, monitor the effectiveness of ventilations. Be careful to give rescue breaths at the usual rate and to not overventilate the victim. Watch for the rise and fall of the victim's chest, and feel for resistance as you squeeze the bag. An increased resistance may mean that there is blood or vomit in the airway, or that the airway is no longer open. A problem can also occur with sealing the mask to the victim's face, especially when a single rescuer must do this with one hand. If air is escaping around the mask, try repositioning the mask and your fingers. If you cannot obtain an adequate seal and the victim's chest does not rise with ventilations, or there are any other problems with using the BVM, then use an alternate technique, such as a resuscitation mask, instead. See the Skill: Bag Mask for Rescue Breathing (2 Rescuers).

If available, supplemental oxygen should be used with the BVM (see the next section). An oxygen reservoir bag is attached to the valve on the bag, and the oxygen tubing attached to the bag **(Figure 9-6)**. The device is used the same way to give ventilations, only now oxygen rather than air is being delivered to the victim. The reservoir holds

Skill: Bag Mask for Rescue Breathing (2 Rescuers)

1 Rescuer 1 assembles the BVM with a mask of the correct size and puts the mask over the victim's mouth and nose.

2 Rescuer 2 positions hands: thumbs and index fingers circling each side of mask, the other three fingers of each hand behind lower jawbone. Pull the jaw up into the mask instead of pushing the mask down on the jaw.

3 Rescuer 2 opens the airway and seals the mask to the victim's face.

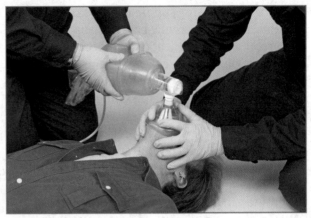

4 Rescuer 1 squeezes the bag to provide ventilations:
   a. 1 ventilation over 1 second in adult, every 5–6 seconds.
   b. 1 ventilation over 1 second in child or infant, every 3–5 seconds.

5 Recheck pulse about every 2 minutes. If no pulse, call for an AED and start CPR.

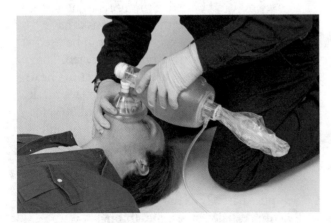

Figure 9-6 A BVM with oxygen reservoir and tubing connected.

oxygen being delivered to the device so that the bag always fills with oxygen to be delivered in the next ventilation. When two rescuers are present, the second sets up the oxygen equipment and prepares to connect it to the BVM while the first begins providing rescue breathing with the BVM alone.

The BVM can be used with a nonbreathing infant in the same manner as with an adult or child. Be sure to choose a mask of the correct size. A smaller bag is also used: typically about 500 mL for newborns, 750 mL for infants and small children, and 1200 mL for large children and adolescents, compared to 1600 mL for adults. Squeeze the bag only enough to make the chest rise, avoiding forceful squeezing or overinflation that may lead to vomiting.

SUPPLEMENTAL OXYGEN

In many emergency situations the victim will benefit from receiving **supplemental oxygen,** if available. Victims receiving basic life support are often receiving insufficient oxygen because of respiratory or cardiovascular problems. The air around us is about 21% oxygen, and the air we breathe out (and into a victim's lungs during rescue breathing) is about 16% oxygen. Depending on the supplemental oxygen delivery device, the victim can receive oxygen at concentrations up to 100%.

Supplemental oxygen, when available, should be used along with other basic life support techniques, including rescue breathing and CPR. In addition, victims with serious medical conditions, including heart attack, stroke, seizures, or serious injury, will potentially benefit from supplemental oxygen.

The following equipment is involved in giving supplemental oxygen:

- The oxygen source is typically a pressurized cylinder. When full, cylinders have a pressure of 2000 pounds per square inch (psi). They come in various sizes and are usually painted green, although some stainless steel cylinders are not.
- The **pressure regulator** reduces the pressure of oxygen leaving the tank to a safe level and has a gauge that shows the pressure remaining within the cylinder. If the gauge reads 2000 psi, the tank is full; if it reads 1000 psi, it is half full; and so on. The pressure regulator is designed so that it works only with oxygen tanks.
- The **flowmeter,** used to adjust the rate of oxygen delivery, is usually built into the pressure regulator. The flow of oxygen reaching the victim is set by turning the calibrated flow valve.
- Oxygen tubing connects the cylinder to the delivery device. Connecting tubes are typically 4 to 5 feet long and have an adapter at each end.
- An **oxygen delivery device,** such as a face mask or nasal cannula, provides the flowing oxygen to the victim.

Safety Around Oxygen

Although oxygen itself does not burn, it vigorously supports combustion and creates a hazardous situation if used near an ignition source. Follow these guidelines around oxygen:

- Never allow smoking or an open flame near the oxygen source.
- Never use grease, oil, or adhesive tape on the cylinder, pressure regulator, or delivery device, because these are combustible.
- Never expose an oxygen cylinder to a temperature above 120° F.
- Never drop a cylinder or let it fall against another object. If the valve is dislodged, the cylinder can become a dangerous projectile powered by the compressed gas.
- Never try to use a non-oxygen regulator on an oxygen cylinder.

Oxygen Delivery Devices

Many different oxygen delivery devices are available, each with certain advantages and disadvantages. The following devices are most frequently used in emergency situations **(Figure 9-7)**:

- **Nasal cannulas,** sometimes called nasal prongs, are used with breathing victims who do not require a high concentration of oxygen. The device has two small prongs that fit shallowly into the nostrils. The nasal cannula is easy to use and comfortable for the victim. The oxygen concentration delivered depends on the flow rate (1 to 6 L/min) and the victim's breathing rate, varying from about 24% to 50%.
- **Resuscitation masks** cover the mouth and nose and can be used for nonbreathing victims receiving rescue breaths. Some masks have a special port for oxygen, which can be used for breathing victims who need oxygen. The mask then can be secured to the victim's head by an elastic band. A typical plastic face mask provides an oxygen concentration of 30% to 60% with a flow rate of 10 liters per minute.
- **Nonrebreathing masks** have a mask and a reservoir bag and are used with breathing victims. The oxygen fills the reservoir, which empties partially as the victim inhales. The victim's exhaled air escapes through a valve. With a minimum oxygen flow rate of 8 liters per

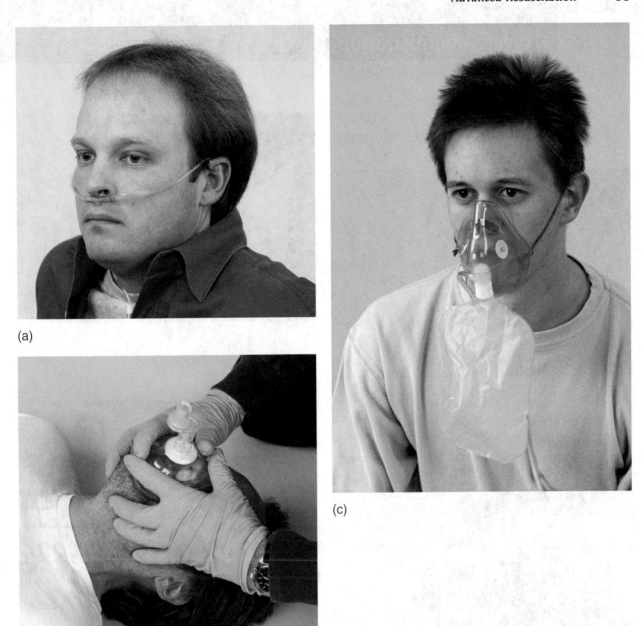

(a)

(b)

(c)

Figure 9-7 Oxygen delivery devices. (a) Nasal cannula. (b) Resuscitation mask. (c) Nonrebreathing mask.

minute, the oxygen concentration ranges from 80% to 95%. The flow rate is adjusted to prevent the reservoir from completely collapsing when the victim inhales. A firm mask fit is needed to prevent atmospheric air from entering the mask.

• **Bag mask units,** as described earlier, can also deliver oxygen either through a simple connecting tube to the bag or with an oxygen reservoir. Oxygen concentrations delivered to a nonbreathing victim by a BVM with a reservoir can approach 100%. A breathing victim can also use a BVM with a reservoir to receive oxygen; unless the victim is having difficulty breathing, the bag is not squeezed.

Skill: **Oxygen Administration**

1   Check equipment: oxygen labels on the cylinder and regulator; tubing and delivery device ready.

2   Remove any protective seal, point the cylinder away, and open the main valve for 1 second.

3   Remove any protective seals and attach the regulator to the oxygen cylinder.

4   Open the main cylinder valve.

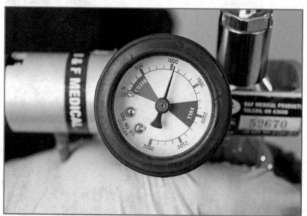

5   Check the pressure regulator gauge.

6   Attach the tubing to the flowmeter and the oxygen delivery device.

Skill: Oxygen Administration (continued)

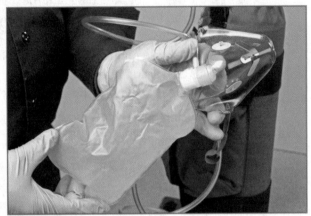

7 Set the flowmeter at the correct oxygen flow rate.
   a. 1–6 L/min for nasal cannula
   b. 10 L/min for face mask
   c. 10–15 L/min for BVM or nonrebreather mask

8 Confirm that the oxygen is flowing.

9 Position the delivery device on the victim and continue rescue breathing (or allow the victim to breathe spontaneously).

10 Monitor the pressure regulator gauge and be prepared to remove the delivery device and change tanks if the pressure drops below 500 psi. Observe oxygen safety precautions.

Administration of Oxygen

The Skill: Oxygen Administration describes the steps for setting up the oxygen equipment and administering oxygen to the victim. Remember to follow safety principles when working with oxygen. If you are alone with a victim, do not stop providing basic life support to set up oxygen equipment. Give rescue breathing or CPR as needed, use the AED if present and appropriate, and care for other life-threatening problems first. Wait until the victim is relatively stable and breathing independently, or until another rescuer can help with the oxygen equipment. Once the victim is receiving oxygen, continue to monitor the flow of oxygen and tank pressure, as well as the victim's condition.

Conclusion

Resuscitation adjunctive devices, when available and when the professional rescuer is trained in their use, increase the efficiency of resuscitation techniques and increase the victim's chances for successful full recovery. Never delay care for a victim, however, in order to get or set up these devices for use.

Case Scenario

On your way home at the end of your shift, you see a crowd on the sidewalk gathered around an older woman who has collapsed. You stop to see if you can help. She is unresponsive, is not breathing, and has no pulse. You immediately radio in for additional help and an AED. You use your pocket mask as you begin providing CPR.

1. After about a minute of CPR, after delivering rescue breaths, the victim vomits. Your best action now is to
   a. Roll the victim onto her side and wait for her mouth to drain clear.
   b. Suction the victim's mouth if you have a suction device.
   c. Continue with chest compressions.
   d. Wait for the AED to arrive.

You continue CPR, and another rescue vehicle arrives on the scene with additional equipment. The first EMT has supplemental oxygen and a BVM, and the second is getting an AED.

2. While the second rescuer is setting up the oxygen equipment, you should—
   a. Continue CPR using your face mask.
   b. Continue CPR using the BVM if you are trained in using it by yourself.
   c. Give chest compressions only until the oxygen tank is set up and the tubing connected to the BVM.
   d. Tell the second rescuer to ignore the oxygen equipment for now and instead assist with two-rescuer CPR.

The second rescuer sets up the equipment, opens the regulator, sets the flowmeter, and connects the oxygen tubing to the BVM. His partner is setting up the AED.

3. What should you be doing at this moment?
   a. Stop CPR and wait for the AED to be ready.
   b. Continue CPR by yourself.
   c. Perform two-rescuer CPR using the BVM connected to oxygen.
   d. Continue CPR and ask the second rescuer to move the oxygen tank 20 feet away before the AED arrives because of the fire hazard.

Appendix A
Review Questions

1. Which pulse should be checked in an infant who is not breathing?
   a. Carotid pulse
   b. Brachial pulse
   c. Posterior tibial pulse
   d. Radial pulse

2. Most AEDs administer a shock to the victim
   a. whenever you turn it on.
   b. automatically after determining the presence of ventricular fibrillation.
   c. when you push the shock button after being prompted to do so.
   d. about 3 seconds after the pads are applied to the victim.

3. A victim with a severe airway obstruction
   a. cannot speak or cough forcefully.
   b. cannot speak but can cough forcefully.
   c. can speak and cough weakly.
   d. can speak but only in short sentences.

4. A bloodborne pathogen can enter the body through
   a. any break in the skin.
   b. food cooked by someone else.
   c. the municipal water supply.
   d. any physical touching of the victim's skin.

5. Assess a victim for responsiveness by
   a. tapping the shoulder and asking if he or she is okay.
   b. pinching the cheek between thumb and forefinger.
   c. checking for pupil reactions to light.
   d. checking skin for normal color and temperature.

6. Advantages of the recovery position include
   a. it lowers the victim's blood pressure.
   b. it allows fluids to drain from the mouth.
   c. it helps prevent shock.
   d. it helps ensure that the brain receives sufficient oxygen.

7. For the purposes of BLS, when does an infant become a child?
   a. At 6 months
   b. At 1 year
   c. At 15 lbs
   d. At 25 lbs

8. Rescue breaths are given with the victim in what position?
   a. On the back
   b. On the side
   c. On the back or the side
   d. In the position in which the victim is found

9. Vomiting during CPR may result from
   a. blowing air in too forcefully.
   b. not blowing enough air in.
   c. compressing the chest too quickly.
   d. compressing the chest too deeply.

10. Preventable risk factors for cardiovascular disease include
    a. race.
    b. low cholesterol levels.
    c. inactivity.
    d. depression.

11. Call for an AED first before beginning CPR for
    a. an unresponsive adult victim who is not breathing.
    b. an unresponsive child or infant who is not breathing.
    c. an unresponsive adult victim with an airway obstruction.
    d. an unresponsive child or infant with an airway obstruction.

12. The hand position for chest compressions depends on
    a. the cause of the victim's cardiac arrest.
    b. the victim's age.
    c. how long the victim has been in cardiac arrest.
    d. the victim's weight.

13. If a victim begins breathing after you have given CPR, what do you do?
    a. Put the victim in the recovery position and monitor breathing
    b. Continue chest compressions and rescue breaths
    c. Continue giving only chest compressions
    d. Give rescue breaths only

14. Bloodborne pathogens are normally transmitted by all these body fluids *except*
    a. semen.
    b. vaginal secretions.
    c. bloody vomit.
    d. urine.

15. If a victim can talk to you, you can be sure he or she
    a. does not have a life-threatening condition.
    b. does not have a spinal injury.
    c. does not have an airway obstruction.
    d. is not having a heart attack.

16. When should you send someone to bring an AED to the scene when you encounter an unresponsive adult?
    a. As soon as you see the victim is unresponsive
    b. As soon as the dispatcher tells you to
    c. After 1 minute of CPR
    d. It depends on the cause of the victim's condition

17. How long should it take to deliver one rescue breath?
    a. ½ second
    b. 1 second
    c. 1½ seconds
    d. 2 seconds

18. When alone, it is acceptable to stop CPR when
    a. ten minutes have passed and the victim has not recovered.
    b. twenty minutes have passed and the victim has not recovered.
    c. you are too exhausted to continue.
    d. the victim feels cold all over.

19. What increases the risk of choking in an adult?
    a. Taking high blood pressure medication
    b. Overcooking foods
    c. Having gum disease
    d. Drinking alcohol with meals

20. What is occurring in ventricular fibrillation?
    a. The ventricles of the heart have stopped moving
    b. The ventricles of the heart are contracting too slowly

    c. The ventricles of the heart are quivering rather than pumping
    d. The ventricles of the heart are contracting with opposing rhythms

21. To open the airway of an unresponsive victim without suspected spinal injury
    a. tilt the head back and lift the chin.
    b. thrust the jaw upward with both hands.
    c. tilt the head back while prying open the mouth.
    d. do not tilt the head back but hold the chin down.

22. What should you *not* do before using an AED?
    a. Ensure that the victim is not breathing and has no pulse
    b. Administer CPR until the AED is ready to use
    c. Turn it on before attaching the pads to the victim
    d. Wipe the victim's chest with an alcohol pad

23. To give abdominal thrusts to a responsive choking adult, what hand position is used?
    a. Both hands together on the bottom edge of the breastbone
    b. Both hands together just above the navel
    c. One hand at the navel and one hand at the "V" where the lower ribs meet
    d. One hand on the bottom rib at each side

24. While the AED is giving the victim a shock, you should
    a. continue CPR.
    b. not touch the victim.
    c. push the shock button repeatedly.
    d. push down on the pads to hold them in place.

25. What is important when giving choking care to a responsive infant?
    a. Alternate series of back slaps and chest thrusts
    b. Keep the infant's head raised above the body
    c. Give CPR in the usual way
    d. Perform a more gentle version of the adult responsive choking technique

26. An AED may be used with a child 1 to 8 years old if
    a. you use a special pediatric unit or pads.
    b. you turn the voltage knob to a lower setting.
    c. you put the pads on the arms to lower the voltage through the heart.
    d. you put petroleum jelly between the skin and the pads.

27. An effective way to avoid becoming infected when caring for a victim is to
    a. ask the victim what diseases he or she may have.
    b. check an unresponsive victim for a medical alert bracelet or necklace.
    c. use barriers to prevent contact with any blood or body fluid.
    d. never touch the victim.

28. What is the correct position for the rescuer's elbows when giving CPR to an adult?
    a. Bent and locked
    b. Straight and locked
    c. Bent and flexible
    d. Straight and flexible

29. The signs and symptoms of heart attack include
    a. chest pain, fever, and flushed skin.
    b. chest pain, headache, and inability to raise both arms.
    c. chest pain, sweating, and shortness of breath.
    d. chest pain, difficulty speaking or swallowing, and vision problems.

30. Which statement is true about the ratio of compressions and breaths when adult CPR is performed by two rescuers?
    a. Rescue breaths are given by one rescuer without the other rescuer pausing in chest compressions
    b. A ratio of 15 compressions and 2 breaths is used for adults
    c. A ratio of 5 compressions and 1 breath is used for adults
    d. The usual ratio of 30 compressions and 2 breaths is used for adults

31. The correct hand position for chest compressions in adults is
    a. on the top of the breastbone below the neck.
    b. on the lower end of the breastbone just above the abdomen.
    c. on the lower half of the breastbone midway between the nipples.
    d. three finger-widths above where the ribs join.

32. What device, if you have it with you and are trained in its use, makes it easier to keep the victim's airway open while providing two-rescuer CPR using a BVM?
    a. Suction
    b. Oxygen
    c. Oral airway
    d. Cricoid pressure

33. For which victim should you provide 5 cycles of CPR before stopping to place a call for an AED?
    a. An adult seen to collapse suddenly
    b. An adult found unresponsive of unknown cause
    c. A child seen to collapse suddenly
    d. An adult pulled from the water

34. Never insert a suction tip into a victim's mouth farther than
    a. you can see.
    b. 3 inches.
    c. 6 inches.
    d. the distance between the victim's eyebrow and corner of the mouth.

35. Which is the correct way to give chest compressions to an infant between breaths in single-rescuer CPR?
    a. Give 15 compressions at a rate of at 80 per minute
    b. Give 15 compressions at a rate of 100 per minute
    c. Give 30 compressions at a rate of 80 per minute
    d. Give 30 compressions at a rate of 100 per minute

36. The oxygen concentration delivered with a BVM with an oxygen reservoir connected to an oxygen source is about
    a. 25%.
    b. 50%.
    c. 80%.
    d. 100%.

37. How long should you check an unresponsive victim for breathing before concluding that he or she is not breathing?
    a. About 2 seconds
    b. No more than 10 seconds
    c. About 20 to 30 seconds
    d. About a minute

38. When using an AED with a victim of hypothermia
    a. briskly rub the victim's chest to warm up the skin below the pads.
    b. handle the victim very carefully.
    c. do not waste time feeling for a pulse.
    d. wait until you have fully warmed the body before applying the pads.

39. A healthcare provider should give an infant or child CPR with chest compressions if there are signs of poor systemic perfusion and the pulse is under
    a. 20 beats per minute.
    b. 40 beats per minute.
    c. 60 beats per minute.
    d. 80 beats per minute.

40. The position for chest compressions in an infant when two healthcare providers are providing CPR is
    a. two fingers just below the line between the nipples.
    b. both thumbs together just below the line between the nipples, with fingers away from chest.
    c. both thumbs together just below the line between the nipples, with fingers encircling the thorax.
    d. both thumbs just below the line between the nipples, with about 2 inches separating the thumbs, and the fingers encircling the thorax.

41. HIV infection can be prevented when giving basic life support by
    a. avoiding all contact with known HIV-positive individuals.
    b. following standard precautions.
    c. getting vaccinated.
    d. wearing a face mask.

42. Which pulse should be checked in an adult victim who is not breathing?
    a. Carotid pulse
    b. Brachial pulse
    c. Femoral pulse
    d. Radial pulse

43. The AED pads should be positioned where on the victim?
    a. Where the diagram on the unit indicates placement
    b. Below the nipples on both sides of the chest
    c. Above the nipples on both sides of the chest
    d. One on the chest and the other on the abdomen

44. Standard precautions include
    a. wearing a face mask with all victims.
    b. using personal protective equipment.
    c. asking a victim about any communicable diseases before giving emergency care.
    d. checking a victim's medical record after giving emergency care.

45. The rate for rescue breathing for an adult victim who has a pulse but is not breathing is
    a. 8 to 10 breaths per minute.
    b. 10 to 12 breaths per minute.
    c. 12 to 16 breaths per minute.
    d. 12 to 20 breaths per minute.

46. If the AED indicates no shock is needed, you should then
    a. wait 20 seconds and try again.
    b. give CPR starting with chest compressions.
    c. remove the pads and turn the AED off.
    d. take the pads off and reposition them.

47. If you cannot successfully open a victim's airway with the jaw thrust
    a. keep trying the jaw thrust with different head positions.
    b. tilt the head back but do not lift the chin.
    c. lift the chin but do not tilt the head back.
    d. use the head tilt–chin lift.

48. Why should a barrier device be used with rescue breaths?
    a. To help get more air into the victim
    b. To prevent vomiting

c. To protect against infectious disease

d. To prevent air from entering the esophagus

49. The correct ratio of chest compressions to breaths for adult CPR given by a single rescuer is

    a. 5 to 2.

    b. 10 to 2.

    c. 15 to 2.

    d. 30 to 2.

50. You respond with an AED to a scene where a 4-year-old child was found unresponsive. He is not breathing and has no pulse. What should you do first?

    a. Use the AED immediately

    b. Give 2 minutes of CPR

    c. Give 6 rescue breaths, then start CPR

    d. Give chest compressions only

Appendix B

Answers to Case Scenarios and Review Questions

Chapter 1

1. Answer choice *d* is the appropriate action to take. Victims who are not aware of the potential seriousness of their condition may at first refuse care but then accept it when they understand the possible consequences. Answer choices *a* and *b* put the victim at greater risk, and the victim has not definitively refused care because he has not yet learned the possible consequences of his actions. Answer choice *c* is inappropriate because Mark does not have the legal right to force the victim to accept care.

2. Answer choice *a* is correct: a professional rescuer must meet the standards of care (what one is trained to do). Because the victim is now unresponsive, Mark now has implied consent to give him lifesaving care such as CPR, and therefore he does not need consent from a family member (this would also be a waste of valuable time in a life-threatening emergency). Because this is a job responsibility, Mark does have a duty (legal obligation) to act.

Chapter 2

1. Answer choice *c* is the appropriate answer: you should put on gloves to prevent exposure to the victim's blood when you touch her to provide care. It is not appropriate to inquire whether she may have an infectious disease—following standard precautions, you should assume that all victims may have one. It is not necessary (and would waste valuable time) to try to clean and disinfect her face before giving care, and coveralls and a face shield are unnecessary because there is little risk of blood splashing on you in this case. (In addition, you should use a face mask when providing rescue breaths.)

2. Answer choice *b* is the best answer. Washing your hands thoroughly is the highest priority to lower the risk of disease transmission; soap and water are the best for washing (unnecessary to soak in bleach solution, which

is used to decontaminate soiled surfaces and equipment). Afterward, you should report the potential exposure to your employer. Followup activities in the exposure control plan may include testing the victim for infectious diseases, and you may be asked to see your physician about possible treatment.

Chapter 3

1. The correct answer choice is *a*. The first step in the ABCs is A for airway. Always perform the ABCs in this order.

2. The appropriate answer choice is *c*. Give two rescue breaths as part of the breathing check (B in the ABCs) because this gets needed oxygen into the victim's lungs and informs you whether the airway is open or potentially obstructed.

3. The correct answer choice is *d*. Remember the ABCs: checking circulation (C) comes after checking breathing (B). Although the victim may need defibrillation, do not wait while the unit is being prepared but complete your initial assessment.

4. The appropriate answer choice is *a*. The victim is not breathing and has no circulation and therefore needs CPR. You will use the AED as soon as it is ready, but until it is, start CPR. (You will learn more about this process in the following chapters.)

Chapter 4

Case A

1. The correct answer is *c*. Ask about medication because she may have a known medical condition that can be helped by medication she may have with her. It is not appropriate to start rescue breathing yet. Although you should ask if she is choking on something, it is not appropriate to give chest compressions while she is still breathing and evidently

has a pulse (this is discussed in Chapter 6). Because respiratory distress may rapidly lead to respiratory arrest, it is not appropriate to simply wait; begin care for the breathing difficulty.

Case B

1. The correct answer is *b*, give him two breaths. This is always the next step when the airway is opened and the victim is found not to be breathing; it gives the victim needed oxygen and helps you determine if the victim is choking. Only after this do you check the pulse and start CPR if needed.

2. The correct answer is *a*, check his pulse. Remember the order of the ABCs—checking circulation (by checking pulse) follows the check of breathing. CPR would be given later, only after establishing that he has no pulse. Abdominal thrusts are inappropriate because this victim does not have an airway obstruction. The recovery position is used only for an unresponsive victim who is breathing and has a pulse.

3. Answer choice *c*. Rescue breathing in an adult is performed at a rate of 1 every 5 to 6 seconds, taking about 1 second to give each breath. You should also check his pulse about every minute.

Chapter 5

Case A

1. The correct answer is *b*, one arm drifting down. This is one of the three signs of stroke revealed by the Cincinnati Prehospital Stroke Scale (the other two are facial droop and difficulty speaking).

2. The correct answer is *b*. Put the victim in the stroke position: lying down on his back with head and shoulders slightly raised. The victim should not eat or drink, and you should not give aspirin or any other drug.

Case B

1. The correct answer is *a*, he may be having a heart attack. Remember, the symptoms are

not always the same. A heart attack victim may not experience crushing chest pain or any chest symptoms at all, and like any other symptom, nausea also may not be present. Never delay care to wait to see if the victim develops additional symptoms, for every minute counts and the risks rise if it takes longer to receive medical care.

2. The correct answer is *a*, help him rest in a position of comfort for easiest breathing. In addition, loosen any constricting clothing, and help him stay calm. Ask if he has any prescribed medication—but you do not administer medication on your own (without specialized training). Do not let the victim eat or drink anything. Be prepared to give BLS if needed.

Case C

1. The correct answer is *c*, start CPR. Give CPR to any victim who is in cardiac arrest. Rescue breathing alone is not enough because she does not have a pulse, and you should not waste time calling the dispatcher again. The recovery position is used only for victims who are breathing and have a pulse.

2. The correct answer is *d*, cycles of 30 compressions and 2 breaths, compressions $1\frac{1}{2}$ to 2 inches deep. The ratio of compressions and breaths differs only for two-rescuer CPR for infants and children (15:2). Chest compression depth in a normal-size adult is always $1\frac{1}{2}$ to 2 inches.

3. The correct answer is *a*, continue with additional cycles of compressions and breaths. Having just checked for a pulse, do not interrupt or delay compressions or change the rate of compressions.

4. The correct answer is *b*, which continues CPR with a smooth transition and no interruptions. Answer choice *a* would interrupt CPR, making it less effective. Answer choice *c* is incorrect because compressions and rescue breaths are given at the same time only if an advanced airway has been inserted.

Chapter 6

1. The correct answer is *a*, give abdominal thrusts because he is a responsive choking victim. You cannot give rescue breathing (if needed) until you clear the airway obstruction. Pounding on the back is generally not an effective technique. CPR is used to clear an airway obstruction in an unresponsive victim.

2. The correct answer is *c*, make sure help has been called—it is crucial to get more help on the way because he may have only minutes to live if you cannot clear the airway obstruction. Then you can check his mouth and give abdominal thrusts. Rescue breathing would be used only once the obstruction is cleared, assuming the victim is still not breathing.

3. The correct answer is *c*, give CPR starting with chest compressions. Pounding on his sternum is not an effective technique, and an AED is likely not needed immediately, since his primary problem is choking. Check his mouth after a series of abdominal thrusts.

Chapter 7

1. The appropriate first step is *a*, open his airway and check for breathing. Even though the circumstances seem to indicate that he has had a heart attack, do not assume that he is not breathing. Remember always to follow the ABCs in order.

2. The correct answer is *c*, provide 5 cycles of CPR (about 2 minutes). He is not breathing and has no pulse, so he needs CPR. Because more than 4 to 5 minutes have passed, give the 2 minutes of CPR before using the AED.

3. The correct answer is *d*, do not touch the victim during the analysis. The victim should not be disturbed during this time. It is appropriate to use the AED now after the first 2 minutes of CPR.

4. The appropriate next step is *b*, continue CPR. This is always done following a shock. You do not need to check for a pulse first. Give 5 cycles of CPR (about 2 minutes) before pausing for the AED to analyze again to determine if another shock is needed.

5. The correct answer is *c*, put him in the recovery position and monitor his breathing and pulse. Because the victim may again experience cardiac arrest, leave the AED pads in place.

Chapter 8

Case A

1. The correct answer is *b*, check for a pulse for up to 30 to 45 seconds. Remember that in severely hypothermic victims, it can be very difficult to detect slow respiratory and heart rates. Start CPR if you have not detected a pulse within 45 seconds. Do not wait for the AED or waste time moving the victim just for rewarming—it is more important to give basic life support first.

2. The correct answer is *a*, use the AED. Follow the standard BLS protocol to use the AED on a victim in cardiac arrest. Stop CPR when the unit is ready to use. After the AED, as time allows, the victim's clothing can be removed to prevent further heat loss. Never try to pump water from a victim's lungs—just give BLS care to victims of submersion as usual.

Case B

1. The correct answer is *c*, make sure the power to the appliance is turned off. Do not touch her to check responsiveness or to check her ABCs until you are sure the risk of electrical shock is eliminated. Do not start CPR until you know she has no pulse.

2. The appropriate next action is *a*, shout for help and give 5 cycles of CPR (about 2 minutes) before telephoning for help if no one comes to the scene. Do not delay CPR to call for or to get an AED—but call after 2 minutes of CPR if she does not revive. The burn on her hand is a lower priority than her life-threatening cardiac arrest.

Chapter 9

1. The best answer is *b*, suction the victim's mouth if you have a suction device. This is the

most effective way to clear the airway. Do not continue CPR until the airway is clear. Never stop CPR and wait for the AED to arrive.

2. The best answer is *b*, continue CPR using the BVM if you are trained in using it by yourself. It is essential to continue CPR, and the victim receives more oxygen through the BVM than the face mask. Do not give only compressions, for the victim needs oxygenation too. Let the second rescuer finish setting up the oxygen equipment and connect the tubing to the BVM to provide supplemental oxygen as CPR continues.

3. The best answer is *c*, perform two-rescuer CPR using the BVM connected to oxygen. Do not stop CPR until the third rescuer has the AED ready to use (until then, two-rescuer CPR is more effective than single-rescuer CPR). It is true that the oxygen should not be used in the presence of a possible ignition source such as a spark, but an AED normally does not present this hazard.

Answers to Review Questions

1. b	14. d	27. c	39. c
2. c	15. c	28. b	40. c
3. a	16. a	29. c	41. b
4. a	17. b	30. d	42. a
5. a	18. c	31. c	43. a
6. b	19. d	32. c	44. b
7. b	20. c	33. d	45. b
8. a	21. a	34. a	46. b
9. a	22. d	35. d	47. d
10. c	23. b	36. d	48. c
11. a	24. b	37. b	49. d
12. b	25. a	38. b	50. b
13. a	26. a		

Glossary

A

abandonment: a type of negligence that occurs if someone who has begun to give care leaves the victim before care is taken over by someone with an equal or higher level of training

ABCs: acronym for airway, breathing, circulation—the three things to check in an unresponsive victim in the initial assessment to find threats to life

acquired immunodeficiency syndrome (AIDS): a fatal disease caused by the human immunodeficiency virus (HIV)

acute myocardial infarction: a condition of dying cardiac muscle tissue caused by a sudden reduced blood flow to the heart muscle; heart attack

advance directive: a legal document signed by an individual, often a terminally ill person, and his or her doctor, that restricts what medical care the person will accept; a living will

advanced cardiac life support (ACLS): medical procedures needed to restore a heartbeat beyond the procedures of basic life support

airborne transmission: transmission of a pathogen from one person to another through the air, usually via small fluid droplets the infected person coughs or sneezes out

airway: a shaped tubelike device inserted into the mouth or nose that helps keep a victim's airway open during resuscitation or until the victim receives advanced medical attention

airway obstruction: a condition in which the victim's airway is partially or completely obstructed by the tongue, vomit or other body tissue or fluids, or a foreign object; choking

angina pectoris: chest pain caused by heart disease; usually occurs after intense activity or exertion; often called angina

aspiration: the movement of vomit or other fluids or solids into the lungs

atherosclerosis: a narrowing and "hardening" of the arteries caused by plaque

B

bag mask (BVM): a resuscitation mask unit connected to a bag that is squeezed to provide air or oxygen to a nonbreathing victim

barrier device: a device, like a pocket mask, used to provide a barrier between the victim and the rescuer when giving rescue breathing to reduce the risk of disease transmission

basic life support (BLS): emergency care given to a victim with a life-threatening problem of the airway or circulation; generally refers to rescue breathing, CPR, and use of an AED

bloodborne transmission: transmission of disease from one person to another through contact with the infected person's blood or certain other body fluids

brachial pulse: the pulse felt over the brachial artery in an infant's upper arm on the inside about midway between the shoulder and elbow

bronchodilator: an inhaled medication used by people with asthma to prevent or control asthmatic attacks

C

call fast: situation in which, when alone with an unresponsive victim, you give 2 minutes of basic life support before pausing to call for an AED

call first: situation in which, when alone with an unresponsive victim, you call for an AED before starting basic life support

cardiac arrest: the sudden stop of the heartbeat

cardiopulmonary resuscitation (CPR): a basic life support procedure for a victim who is not breathing and has no heartbeat, consisting of rescue breathing combined with chest compressions

carotid pulse: the pulse felt over the carotid artery in the neck of an adult or child

chain of survival: a concept emphasizing four steps needed for cardiac arrest victims: early access, early CPR, early defibrillation, and early advanced medical care

cholesterol: a fatty substance the body needs to carry out important functions but that in high levels is a risk factor for cardiovascular disease

Cincinnati Prehospital Stroke Scale (CPSS): a screening process for rapid identification of a stroke outside the hospital

competent: the victim is able to understand what is happening and the implications of his or her decision to receive or refuse emergency care

confidentiality: the general principle that one should not give out private information about a victim to anyone except for those caring for the victim

consent: the victim's permission for a trained rescuer to provide emergency care

coronary artery disease: blockage of vessels supplying heart muscle with blood, often leading to heart attack

cricoid pressure: a technique of applying pressure to an area of cartilage in the neck to prevent the air given during rescue breathing from reaching the stomach; also called the Sellick maneuver

critical incident stress debriefing: a formal program in many organizations and facilities to assist those experiencing the effects of stress after an emergency

D

decontamination: the use of physical or chemical means to remove, inactivate, or destroy bloodborne pathogens on a surface or item so that it is no longer infectious

defibrillation: the process of administering an electrical shock to a fibrillating heart to restore a normal heart rhythm

direct contact: disease transmission that occurs when someone directly contacts an infected person, or fluids or substances from that person

disinfectant: a substance, such as a bleach solution, that kills most pathogens on contaminated surfaces

dispatcher: an EMS professional who answers 9-1-1 calls, determines the nature of the emergency, and sends the appropriate emergency personnel to the scene

Do Not Resuscitate (DNR) order: a specific kind of advance directive that indicates the ill person has chosen not to be resuscitated if his or her heart and breathing stop

duty to act: the legal obligation to care for a victim of a medical emergency, accepted as a dimension of a trained professional's job description

E

electrodes: the pads of an automated external defibrillator, which attach to the main unit with cables and deliver the shock to a victim's chest when indicated

Emergency Medical Services (EMS) system: a comprehensive network of professionals linked together to provide appropriate levels of medical care for victims of injury or sudden illness

emergency medical technician (EMT): emergency personnel trained to give prehospital medical treatment to injured or ill victims and to transport victims to advanced care facilities

engineering controls: devices that isolate or remove the bloodborne pathogen hazard

EpiPen®: a commercially available emergency epinephrine kit for use by those experiencing severe allergic reactions to bee stings, certain foods, etc.

exposure control plan: a plan employers must have in place to prevent exposure to bloodborne pathogens

expressed consent: consent explicitly given by the victim for emergency care

F

femoral pulse: the pulse felt in the center of the groin crease

fibrillation: an abnormal heart rhythm in which muscles of the heart are quivering instead of beating rhythmically; see *ventricular fibrillation*

first responder: the first trained professional rescuer to arrive at the emergency scene

flowmeter: a device, usually built into the oxygen pressure regulator, used to adjust the rate of oxygen delivery to the victim

G

Good Samaritan law: a state law designed to protect people from being sued for giving emergency care

H

Heimlich maneuver: abdominal thrusts given to a responsive choking victim to expel the obstructing object

hepatitis: the various forms of liver disease caused by the bloodborne hepatitis B virus (HBV), hepatitis C virus (HCV), or other hepatitis viruses

human immunodeficiency virus (HIV): the virus that causes AIDS

hypertension: high blood pressure

I

implied consent: consent that a rescuer can assume is given to administer emergency care to an unresponsive victim or a child without a parent or guardian present

inadequate breathing: such slow breathing that oxygen levels in the blood are dropping to life-threatening levels

indirect contact: disease transmission through contact with contaminated objects, food or drink, droplets in the air, or vectors such as insects

initial assessment: a quick first check of the victim for life-threatening problems, involving a check for responsiveness and the ABCs

M

medical direction: the process by which EMS personnel and some professional rescuers are guided in certain medical interventions in the field by a physician

meningitis: a contagious viral or bacterial infection of the fluid surrounding the spinal cord and brain

N

nasal cannula: nasal prongs that deliver oxygen to breathing victims who do not require a high concentration of oxygen

nasopharyngeal airway: a nasal airway inserted through the nose and into the pharynx

negligence: a breach of duty, when one has a duty to act, that results in injury or damages to a victim

nitroglycerin: a prescription medication for angina and heart attack that increases blood flow through partially restricted coronary arteries

nonrebreathing mask: an oxygen delivery device consisting of a mask and a reservoir bag, used with breathing victims

O

Occupational Exposure to Bloodborne Pathogens Standard: a set of regulations from the Occupational Safety and Health Administration (OSHA) designed to protect employees from exposure to bloodborne disease pathogens

oropharyngeal airway: an oral airway inserted through the mouth and into the pharynx

oxygen delivery device: a device, such as a face mask or nasal cannula, that provides the flowing oxygen to the victim

P

pacemaker: a small electronic device, implanted under the skin in some patients with heart disease, that helps the heart maintain a regular rhythm

personal protective equipment (PPE): barriers such as gloves and resuscitation masks that prevent being exposed to blood and other body fluids when caring for a victim in an emergency or working around potentially infected materials

pressure regulator: a device attached to an oxygen tank that reduces the pressure of oxygen to a safe level; includes a gauge showing the pressure remaining within the tank

professional rescuer: a trained person who, in either an employment or a volunteer situation, has the responsibility to provide emergency care when needed; in this text, the professional rescuer is assumed to be trained to the level of a "healthcare provider BLS rescuer" by 2005 standards

pulse: a regular pulsing sensation felt over the victim's artery at the neck (adult or child) or upper arm (infant) that signifies the heart is beating and the victim has circulation

R

recovery position: a position used for breathing, unresponsive victims while waiting for help to arrive; the victim is positioned on the side to keep the airway open and allow fluids to drain from the mouth

rescue breathing: a technique for getting air or oxygen into a nonbreathing person's lungs to oxygenate the blood

respiratory arrest: a condition in which breathing has completely stopped

respiratory distress: a condition in which the victim's breathing is difficult

resuscitation: a general term referring to the procedures used in an attempt to restore breathing and/or circulation to a victim

resuscitation mask: a device that covers the mouth and nose of nonbreathing victims to provide rescue breaths

risk factor: anything that makes it more likely that a person will develop a particular disease

S

scope of practice: actions one is trained and qualified to perform, such as specific basic life support skills performed by professional rescuers

secondary assessment: an assessment performed after determining that the victim does not have life-threatening problems, including obtaining a history and performing a physical examination

sharps: any devices or items that may accidentally cut a person handling them, such as needles, scissors, scalpels, and broken glassware

sinus rhythm: the normal rhythm of the heart

standard precautions: a set of safety guidelines for treating all blood and other potentially infectious materials as if known to be contaminated

standards of care: how emergency care should be performed; what others with the same training would do in a similar situation

sterilize: to use a chemical or physical procedure to destroy all microbial life on an item

sternum: the breastbone

stoma: a hole in the neck used for breathing that was surgically created as a result of an injury or illness

stroke: an interruption of blood flow to a part of the brain; also called a cerebrovascular accident (CVA) or brain attack

suction device: a mechanical, electrical, or oxygen-powered device used to clear blood, vomit, and other substances from a victim's airway

sudden illness: any medical condition that occurs suddenly and requires emergency care

sudden infant death syndrome (SIDS): a condition, whose exact cause is poorly understood, that results in an apparently otherwise healthy infant dying suddenly in its sleep

supplemental oxygen: oxygen, usually from a tank, delivered to victims in many emergency situations

T

transient ischemic attack (TIA): a temporary interruption to blood flow in an artery in the brain; sometimes called a mini-stroke

tripod position: a position often assumed by a victim with respiratory distress: sitting, leaning forward with hands on knees

tuberculosis (TB): a highly contagious airborne disease caused by bacteria

U

universal precautions: safety guidelines for treating blood and certain human body fluids as if they are known to be infectious for bloodborne pathogens; the term is generally being replaced by the term *standard precautions*

V

vector transmission: transmission of a bloodborne pathogen from an infected person or animal through the bite of a tick, mosquito, or other insect

ventricular fibrillation (V-fib): an abnormal heart rhythm, which commonly occurs during heart attacks, in which the ventricles of the heart are quivering instead of beating rhythmically

W

work practice controls: specific methods of working around blood or other infectious material that reduce the risk for disease transmission

Index